CONSCIOL

MW01011707

"Sometimes it takes a mountain-moving event to acknowledge that someone has a unique ability and timeless wisdom to spark an inner fire and energize us to remember the core genius truth of who we are. That someone is Sarah Mane. Sarah provides a proposition for us to move beyond the limitations of past conditioning and outdated beliefs and realize the truth that we are magnificent universal beings. This is the timeless wisdom of Sanskrit in its very fluency and perfection in the very essence of igniting genius possibilities. *Conscious Confidence* is a manifest for success in times of chaos and a knowing that—energized as universal transformation and belief awakening—rises up to remind us that it is our birthright to achieve our highest ideals and to imagine we can do extraordinary things because we are extraordinary."

— **DR. PAT BACCILI, Ph.D.,** speaker, author, host of The Dr. Pat Show, and founder of the Transformation Talk Radio Network

"There are a lot of self-development books in the marketplace these days, and there are a lot of authors writing them, but rarely do you find an author with Sarah Mane's depth of understanding. It can only come from a lifetime of unwavering commitment to living a life based on the deep insights embodied in the world's great wisdom traditions. *Conscious Confidence* is not only a book to acquaint the reader with these philosophical insights but is, more importantly, full of practical ways to reap the benefits that can only come with applying them. Like a thirsty person lost in the desert of worldly existence, drink deeply of the wisdom contained in this book."

— **DR. CRAIG HAASED, MD, OAM** (Order of Australia Medal for Services to Medicine and Health), coauthor of *Mindfulness for Life*, and author of *The Freedom Trap: Reclaiming Liberty and Wellbeing* and *New Frontiers in Medicine: The Body as the Shadow of the Soul*

"Sanskrit is regarded as a sacred language, said to be the language used by the soul. But it is much more than that. Sanskrit has the power to open the many chambers of our heart and connect us with the inner sacred dimensions of our being. The complex structure and grammar of Sanskrit can refine the mind and bring clarity of thought and a deeper understanding of the flow of consciousness, the universe at large, and the reality of individual lives on this planet. In *Conscious Confidence* Sarah Mane offers a spiritual and conscious framework for achieving balance in your life and shows you how to weave colorful new threads into your destiny."

— **LIANE BUCK,** editor of *Om Times*

"*Conscious Confidence* is more than a review of Sanskrit practices. Mane takes these lessons and weaves them into larger life goals and a confidence-boosting program designed to apply to all walks of people in different stages of their spiritual or life journeys. This creates an environment of positive thinking and reflection that forms the foundation of a treatise that is flexible enough to be applied to many situations on many different levels. Because life delivers many blows and challenges to such positive thinking, *Conscious Confidence* delivers an especially powerful message that encourages readers to constantly examine their perceptions and impulses to adopt a calmer countenance and make choices based not on reaction but on maintaining better balance."

— **DIANE DONOVAN,** *California Bookwatch*

Use the Wisdom of Sanskrit
to Find Clarity and Success

SARAH MANE

FINDHORN PRESS

Findhorn Press
One Park Street
Rochester, Vermont 05767
www.findhornpress.com

Text stock is SFI certified

Findhorn Press is a division of Inner Traditions International

Disclaimer
The information in this book is given in good faith and intended for information only. Neither author nor publisher can be held liable by any person for any loss or damage whatsoever which may arise from the use of this book or any of the information therein.

Cataloging-in-Publication data for this title is available from the Library of Congress

ISBN 978-1-62055-955-0 (print)
ISBN 978-1-62055-956-7 (ebook)

Printed and bound in the United States by Lake Book Manufacturing, Inc. The text stock is SFI certified. The Sustainable Forestry Initiative® program promotes sustainable forest management.

10 9 8 7 6 5 4 3 2 1

Edited by Michael Hawkins
Text design and layout by Richard Crookes
This book was typeset in Avenir Next, Bliss, Bliss Small Caps, Sanskrit Pro

To send correspondence to the author of this book, mail a first-class letter to the author, c/o Inner Traditions • Bear & Company, One Park Street, Rochester, VT 05767, USA, and we will forward the communication, or contact the author directly at **https://consciousconfidence.com**

—◆—

To Leon MacLaren,
teacher and guide who lit the way
with timeless wisdom.

And to my beloved husband, Gilbert,
ever-present inspiration.

—◆—

"Life falls from Self as shadow falls from Man.
Life and Self are interwoven."

—Shrī Purohit Swāmi and W. B. Yeats,
Prashna Upanishad, The Ten Principal Upanishads

◆

"This above all: to thine own self be true…"

—William Shakespeare,
Hamlet (Act 1, Scene 3)

CONTENTS

INTRODUCTION

We are in truth limitless, magnificent universal beings. Right here and now, we embody all the forces of the universe. There is no difference between our energy and the energy of the universe; they are one and the same. All the wisdom traditions tell us this simple truth.

In this book I will be drawing on the wisdom of the ancient language of Sanskrit. This language, used by the sages of India to write their poetry, epics and works of profound wisdom, is an incomparable tool for delving into the truest knowledge. Sanskrit is not just a language to be written and spoken but is also a doorway to gaining understanding of our experience of life and truth.

The timeless wisdom of Sanskrit restates and re-emphasizes the simple truth that we are universal. While our ordinary experience may be one of limitation, throughout time all the wisdom traditions tell us that the limits we feel are imagined and superimposed on that limitless universal self. This book draws on wisdom not only from Sanskrit but also from other traditions, both East and West. You will learn from the pre-eminent Sanskrit scholar and sage Pāṇini, the *Upanishads,* the *Bhagavad Gītā,* Plato, Shakespeare, and Homer, the Ancient Greek poet. In fact, the same wisdom is available wherever we look. In this book I will show how it is still relevant today and how it can have a beneficial effect on our everyday life.

Opportunities and freedoms abound for us to express that universal energy in our own unique and individual way and to live a glorious life with purpose and passion. Innovation and developments, in fields such as technology, transport and medicine, have made many improvements in lifestyle. These improvements are widely available. They have made daily living so much easier than even one hundred years ago. Truly we live in changing and exciting times.

One interesting aspect of these changing times is how many of us are questioning the traditions of the past. These traditions and values provided certainty, confidence and consistency to many generations. They had an important and stabilizing function in our lives and our society. However, they are now running out of energy and momentum. Their relevance is under question resulting in a lack of faith in our institutions and in ourselves.

There is nothing inherently wrong with this; it is all very natural. However, these shifts are not always comfortable.

History shows that there have been many natural cycles of human consciousness over the millennia. For example, classical civilizations gave way to the Dark Ages and then to the Renaissance. As one phase undergoes dissolution, it leaves the space for something new to arise: a new awareness, a new consciousness, a new foundation.

Right now, we are living through a time of societal change. If we lack strong and lasting foundations in our lives, we can feel uncertain and vulnerable. It can seem as if there is nothing upon which to rely. We might wonder what the use of trusting anything is, if it is soon going to change.

With all this perpetual change comes the shadow of anxiety and fear that hangs low over people in the 21st-century. Rapidly changing and evolving technology provides constant distraction, and this numbs the pain of fear. Lives full of promise are frittered away, but this needn't be us. This doesn't have to happen!

It is time for us to establish new foundations, so we can express our full potential free from the barriers of fear. These foundations need to be established deep within ourselves.

The underpinnings of a house support the whole structure. So, too, we need to build a firm internal foundation to achieve certainty, clarity, and success. These inner foundations are not necessarily visible. They are woven from strength, confidence and self-knowledge. They show themselves in our actions, in our speech and in our attitude to life.

Without proper foundations, the forces of nature large and small destabilize a building. Without proper foundations, a storm or shifts in the ground eventually make a building fall. The lack of proper foundations renders the building susceptible to external forces and unable to stand on its own.

How do we build strong foundations within ourselves?
We do this by firmly establishing our conscious awareness deep within our true being: the heart of who we truly are. It is there that we discover the core values and principles upon which our life is built.

For years, many of us have searched for the answers to life mastery outside ourselves, looking for foundations to give us strength, resilience, confidence and certainty. Many people turn to science and psychology to provide explanations to solve their problems. Now, however, people are awakening to the realization that there are some mysteries that remain beyond the scope of these disciplines. We have to look elsewhere. Something more is required: something that doesn't change, is powerful, and has stood the test of time. Something timeless indeed.

By following this timeless wisdom, we discover something universal, unchanging and all-powerful within us. This is the real source of our confidence in this ever-changing world. Through this unchanging source within ourselves, we realize how to live happily, peacefully, abundantly and successfully. We can then embrace new opportunities that come with change and transition, and with a confidence and certainty that doesn't go away.

Fortunately, an unbroken thread of conscious wisdom that stretches from the past to today is readily available to anyone who wants it. Wise men and women throughout the ages have formulated this wisdom for us. Their purpose has been to connect humanity with a universal source of timeless knowledge regardless of changing circumstances. The ancient and beautiful language of Sanskrit is one expression of this unbroken thread. Sanskrit hasn't changed over time; it is full and complete, and it retains its potency and the purity of its wisdom.

People from all walks of life—from Hollywood celebrities to local café servers—have begun to find that Sanskrit holds out a promise of something powerful, new and beautiful. Perhaps it's the shape of the script, or the beauty of the sound, or a connection to the deep wisdom of a word, phrase or passage that wins their devotion. They may not realize how meaningful the Sanskrit words are. They may simply be attracted to the ideas behind the beautiful Sanskrit script.

Jessica Alba is just one celebrity who has a Sanskrit tattoo. She has the word "padma" tattooed on her wrist. This word means "lotus," and this flower stands as a symbol of spiritual beauty and also the ability to remain pure in the face of the heartache and shortcomings of worldly life.

There are other famous examples. Musicians such as Tina Turner and Madonna have experienced major transformations. Celebrities such as these often turned pain and suffering to freedom, joy and love through reaching into the limitless well-spring of true wisdom with Sanskrit and meditation.

There are many recordings of beautiful Sanskrit mantras, and they even appear in theme music for movies such as *Star Wars, Battlestar*

Galactica, and *The Matrix.* Celebrity tattoos, wedding band engravings, and movie themes in Sanskrit are all indications of people's desire to remain connected with this deep and constant wisdom which brings meaning and fulfillment.

The search continues for how to integrate this ancient timeless wisdom into our contemporary 21st century lives; how we can awaken to lasting meaning, love, joy and fulfillment.

The aim of this book is to welcome you to the world of Conscious Confidence, a practical way to use the wisdom of Sanskrit to find clarity and success. By reading this book, you are connecting to a thread of timeless wisdom that has guided humanity throughout the millennia. Opinions, viewpoints and attitudes come and go, but this golden cord of conscious wisdom is ever-fresh, relevant and powerful. It is wisdom upon which we can utterly depend.

Conscious Confidence is like a great tree with deep strong roots, able to withstand storms and tempests and also provide shelter, stability and nourishment. It is grounded yet continually growing, expanding and evolving. Sanskrit and timeless wisdom help us to plant that tree properly and deepen those roots. Conscious Confidence is the confidence you have when you live boldly and courageously from a commitment to giving the best of your own unique self-expression to the world. It is the confidence you experience when you are awake and aware of your own potential and strength.

I've been fortunate enough to study and practice timeless wisdom for most of my life. I grew up in an ordinary suburban home with my parents and siblings; from the outside there was nothing special. From the inside however, it was extraordinary. My parents were keen seekers of self-knowledge back in the 1960s. I was interested in their enthusiastic discussions at home; they had clearly discovered something that really mattered, and I wanted that too. So, I followed them and joined practical philosophy classes when I was ten years old in 1971.

What do I mean by practical philosophy? The word "philosophy" comes from Ancient Greek and means "love of wisdom"; "philo" means "love," and "sophos" means "wisdom." Notice I said "practical" philosophy, not theoretical. We learnt and studied, and we also practiced. The purpose of the practice was to discover for ourselves the meaning of what was under discussion. Only through direct experience can a person really know and transcend theory. This was how the foundations were established deep within myself.

In our practical philosophy classes, we studied ancient timeless wisdom from many traditions, practiced meditation twice a day, and studied Sanskrit. The approach was always to discover its meaning in practical daily life, not just on special occasions. This set a direction for my whole life, especially throughout my later careers as a teacher and executive coach.

Timeless wisdom resonated with me from the start. It was so simple and practical. I grew up trusting this; it established the strength, anchor and roots within myself.

Take a simple direction such as, "Fall still and remember who you really are." Students in these practical philosophy classes were encouraged to apply this in daily life by coming into the present moment, where everything became clear and calm. All concerns, thoughts and problems fell away, despite what might be happening around us.

This was incredibly powerful and really handy as I grew up, especially through the usual ups and downs of the teenage years. I would often repeat some Sanskrit in my mind when I didn't know what to do next or if I felt confused. I became centered and steady; it brought me back to peace and self-presence. I learnt from experience that this was how to be grounded.

In my adult life I have come to realize that this is the only way to live; by following easy, simple, practical and yet profound timeless wisdom. I found it a blessing of untold power and grace. I also came to see that many people who yearn for a little stillness and peace in their lives don't know where to find it. It's ever-present and yet the one place we don't look is right under our own nose! Sometimes, when it is found, it can be forgotten. I began to wonder how timeless wisdom can be passed on to those who want it, in such a way that it sticks, that it becomes part of their lived experience.

I've had the good fortune to pass on the timeless wisdom of Sanskrit to children and adults throughout my teaching and coaching work. As decades have passed, I have seen time and again how even a little of this consciousness, presence and wisdom is utterly transformative.

Over time, I developed an effective method of teaching this timeless wisdom.

Our life is an expression of what we hold in our heart—of our understanding of things and their meaning. This book is designed for you to consciously redefine those meanings and discover new dimensions of understanding and awareness from the depths of Sanskrit wisdom. This will awaken you to your potential, your core values and what's really important in life. With the ancient wisdom of Sanskrit, you can learn how to transform pain and suffering to joy, freedom and fulfillment.

For the most part we are unaware of the meaning and significance that we give to the events, objects and people in our lives. These meanings are a collection of stories we've gathered, usually unconsciously throughout childhood. This is quite natural. By referring to the timeless wisdom held in Sanskrit, we can apply our conscious intelligence to clarify our thinking and find true meaning. This expands our outlook beyond our stories from the past, allowing us to see new possibilities and opportunities. This leads to success. In whatever way we define the word "success," it means we achieve our goals, whatever they are, and live a life filled with happiness, meaning and purpose.

The approach of this book is simple and practical. The alternative is complex and useless, and, in these circumstances, success is elusive. We fall back into old patterns that no longer work for us, rather than transforming our lives according to our desires. This book will:

- present new definitions and beautiful meanings of profound concepts and ideas that are derived from Sanskrit and the ancient wisdom traditions;
- provide simple analogies that will help your understanding;
- demonstrate the application of timeless wisdom through a mix of delightful traditional and contemporary stories;
- teach you powerful exercises that will help you easily engage with timeless wisdom yourself. This is what I did, and you will also come to know without doubt that it works.

The chapters in this book generally have the following elements:

- a quote of timeless wisdom;
- a brief explanation of what the chapter is about;
- a story or two from a wisdom tradition;

- definitions of the Sanskrit word or words related to the topic at hand and a deeper meaning to expand your understanding;
- a contemporary story to help you see how to apply timeless wisdom to everyday life;
- practices including a starter practice, at least one intermediate practice, and an advanced practice.

Why Sanskrit?

I've been studying and practicing philosophy and self-development for most of my life. I had a natural inclination and desire for it. I always wanted to know what was really going on. I'm also drawn to whatever is useful and practical. Some may wonder how Sanskrit fits into this. They might think Sanskrit is simply an ancient language. It is more than that, for the words carry timeless wisdom that can be accessed when we look into their deeper meanings.

Sanskrit has been useful every day of my life, enhancing my teaching, coaching and ordinary living. Even while washing up the dishes with attention and joy, I am applying a simple principle of timeless wisdom that is embedded in Sanskrit. Studying this wisdom literature immediately opens up a new world of experience.

For decades, I attended formal classes of disciplined study and practice of philosophy, meditation and Sanskrit. The aim was always full self-realization and to raise the level of consciousness of humanity. Starting at such a young age meant that I've always seen this as completely normal and natural.

As a young adult, whilst continuing to study and practice, I tutored many adult philosophy groups as well. Passing on what I'd learnt and experienced was a natural development. The opportunity to guide other seekers was a privilege and an honor. This gave me an insight and breadth of experience in assisting men and women through the various challenges in their lives as they sought to bring timeless universal principles into their experience. Studying Sanskrit at university was a logical extension. It broadened my knowledge and appreciation even further.

For thirty years I taught in a children's school founded on these very same philosophical principles. I was closely involved with all aspects of the school's development and management, including the introduction of the first Sanskrit curriculum for children. I trained teachers and taught the students. Sanskrit and mindfulness for children were, and still are, core subjects in that school's curriculum. This considerably deepened my knowledge, practice and experience of philosophical principles, meditation and Sanskrit.

Decades of tutoring groups of adult seekers of wisdom and self-realization, together with teaching children and working with their parents, and latterly also my executive coaching work, have given me a distinctive skill-set. They have qualified me to speak, write and teach on this subject of developing confidence and certainty through timeless wisdom in an ever-changing and evolving world.

In my life and career, I have sought to learn and teach unchanging universal principles which can be applied at all times and in all circumstances. Principles such as: Everything begins in stillness. Love your neighbour as yourself. Recognize the power of the present moment.

The hallmark of universal principles such as these is that they are always relevant and up-to-date, and they embody timeless wisdom.

The other characteristic of universal principles is they are simple, and you don't need too many of them. The modern world seems weighed down with a myriad of ever-changing highly detailed rules and regulations on every topic under the sun.

One of the main aims of this book is to help you cut through to a more fundamental wisdom which is the foundation to an unchanging Conscious Confidence.

Change can be very exciting, but it can also bring up insecurity, doubts and fear as we are left on our own to discover who we are and what to do. I have worked with hundreds of men and women, young and not so young, who have been troubled by these challenges. These seekers are looking for certainty in a fluid world. Some of their questions are:

- How can I find happiness?
- Do I have enough confidence in myself to follow my heart's true desire?
- Where can I find peace?
- How can I fit everything into a busy day and a busy life?
- What can I do to de-stress?
- How can I succeed and still be myself?
- What is truly important to me?

- How can I balance my own needs and the needs of others?
- How can I find the confidence in myself to embrace new, interesting opportunities?
- How do I trust and believe in myself?

This book also addresses the big questions such as "Who am I?" and "What is the meaning of my life?" and "How can I create value in my own life and in the lives of others?"

With just a little knowledge and application, we will discover our own "Ah-ha!" moments as we find our own answers to all of these questions and more.

In a marketplace of ideas that can appear complex and confusing, my approach is to keep things to a few simple principles that are true, dependable and have been tested over millennia. The alternative is to fill the space with lots of detailed rules and regulations, which seem to change with every passing fashion. I have found that this approach makes my own life so much easier and happier, and my fervent wish is to help you simplify your life and find new meaning and fulfillment as well.

I have tried to make this book entertaining and readable, full of stories, references to timeless wisdom from Sanskrit, and inspiring contemporary accounts of people discovering hidden depths in their own life. It has practical exercises that anyone can do, practices that are powerful and transformative.

This book outlines an effective practical program—the F.U.S.E. Program—which helps establish a safe and secure inner reference point from which to see the world, and from which to make clear decisions on how to act, what to say and how to feel.

Best of all this book offers certainty: It will transform your life.

Chapter One

SANSKRIT, TIMELESS WISDOM, AND PRACTICE

"May Life, Master of the three worlds,
protect us as a mother protects her children.
Grant us wisdom, grant us luck."

—Shrī Purohit Swāmi and W. B. Yeats,
Prashna Upanishad, The Ten Principal Upanishads

In this chapter, I will cover the three key elements of Conscious Confidence: Sanskrit, Timeless Wisdom, and Practice.

Sanskrit, the ancient Indian language of spirituality, scripture and profound philosophy, will be our constant guide and reference point throughout this book. When I look at any new concept the first question is: What does Sanskrit teach us? I will also link that deep meaning of Sanskrit to other sources of Timeless Wisdom such as Plato, Shakespeare, the myths of Ancient Greece, and many others. The third element is Practice. Timeless wisdom goes deep when we take what is said and put it into practice in our daily life.

The story you are about to read is from the *Katha Upanishad*. The Upanishads are also known as the Vedānta because they are the sacred spiritual writings at the end (anta) of the Vedas. They are part of the profound Indian wisdom tradition. The word "Upanishad" means "to sit down near to" the source of wisdom, and then to hear it.

Nachiketas and the Lord Yama

Vājashravas, a clever and wealthy man, decided he wanted to ensure that he would attain heaven when it was time for him to die. He arranged for a special sacrifice to be performed. It was a huge and grand occasion, and many priests gathered to officiate for him. Special gifts had to be prepared too.

Vājashravas offered many gifts to the priests, so he could gain favour in the eyes of the gods. However, he only gave away his old cows who could no longer produce milk or bear calves. He kept back the best cows for himself.

◆

Vājashravas had a son called Nachiketas. He was a steady young man. Nachiketas observed his father's behaviour, and despite his youth, realized that if his father really wanted to attain heaven, then this was not going to happen with his dishonest actions.

Nachiketas remaining calm and without judgment, simply asked him:

"Dear father, have you also given me away to the gods?"
His father was so preoccupied with his grand show of gift-giving, that Nachiketas asked the same question a second, and even a third time.

Vājashravas, not wanting to be diverted from his dealings, turned to his son and snapped, "I give you to the Lord of Death — God Yama!"

Nachiketas was quite indifferent to this surprising answer. He thought, "All things in this world are temporary. I have no fear. I want to know what lies beyond this experience of life."

◆

Vājashravas, now realized what he had done. He hadn't really meant it, he had spoken hastily out of anger and irritation, he didn't want his son to go to the realm of Death.

Nachiketas, however, followed the principle that "a man's word is his bond."

He said, "Father, our revered ancestors have never gone back on their word, and I don't want you to do so either. I understand that following the path of truth is the only way to heaven. I shall go to the abode of the great god—Lord Yama."

With that, he clasped his hands together, bowed to his unhappy father and left.

◆

Nachiketas arrived at Lord Yama's home, only to find that Lord Yama wasn't there. So, Nachiketas patiently sat on the doorstep and began to meditate. After three days, Yama returned home only to find this young man quietly meditating at the entrance.

Yama was concerned. It was an ancient custom that a guest should be offered hospitality, water, food and a seat. Yama had not been there to do this for his unexpected guest, and so had failed to fulfill his duty.

Yama greeted Nachiketas with great respect and said, "I have kept you waiting for three days without a proper welcome of water, food, a seat or any hospitality. By way of recompense, I offer you three special gifts of your choosing. Ask for anything. I beg you to free me from my transgression."

Nachiketas graciously replied, "For my first gift, I wish to be reconciled with my father, so that he may be happy again, and bear no ill-will towards me and make me welcome in his house once more when I return from your abode."

Yama happily granted this first wish.

Nachiketas then said, "Sir, for my second wish, I desire to know how to reach the realm of heaven where there is no sorrow, fear, old age or death." Nachiketas asked this, not for himself but for all people, and especially for his father. He wanted everyone to know this secret wisdom, so they could be free from suffering. Yama was pleased at the selflessness of Nachiketas. His young student listened intently as he, the great Lord Yama—god of Death, spoke:

"There is a Fire, within the heart of every person, that leads to heaven. This is where one is free from fear, sorrow, old age and death." Yama was encouraged to continue by Nachiketas' diligence and attention.

"This Fire is three-fold, comprised of knowledge, meditation and practice." Yama continued to teach Nachiketas of this triple Fire, which once kindled within the heart, leads to heaven.

He concluded, "As you have pleased me, I give you another gift. I shall name this triple Fire after you; hereafter it will be called the Nachiketas Fire. Now tell me what is your third and final gift?"

"Some people say that one exists after death, and some say that one does not," said Nachiketas. "Please explain; I want to learn from you, Lord Yama—the great god of Death. That is my third gift."

Yama was reluctant to answer this very difficult question. He repeatedly offered Nachiketas all manner of riches, honours, power and wealth. Every great and glorious thing was presented to entice him to change his mind and choose another gift. However, Nachiketas was unmoved.

◆

"All these things that you offer are temporary," said Nachiketas. "All riches, glories, power and possessions will eventually pass away. How can anyone be truly satisfied by that alone? My choice of gift is unchanged; what happens to a soul when the body is left behind?"

Yama, then laid out two diverging paths. One is the path of ignorance, which those with limited vision delight in following. It is paved with fleeting pleasures, petty victories and meaningless defeats. The other is the path of Timeless Wisdom, where the seeker of truth acquires the knowledge of the in-dwelling, all-knowing Self, and finally attains a place of strength, a place of peace, a place of confidence, a place of fulfillment.

This particular story is about a young boy who was intent on learning timeless wisdom and would not accept anything less.

Everyone faces these two roads at every moment of their life. Everyone is completely free to choose either the way of awareness, confidence and truth, or they can find themselves going down a different path. The choice is simple, but the consequences are profound. If one has knowledge, guidance and access to simple effective practices, then it is much easier to consistently choose the path of wisdom.

You, too, can follow Nachiketas and choose the path of wisdom. Before we get started on that path, we need to look at the three key elements that underpin this book: Sanskrit, other timeless wisdom traditions, and practice.

The Power of Sanskrit

The word "sanskrita" (संस्कृत) means "purified and perfectly formed."

It is said that Sanskrit is the language of the universe. The wise say, that when all the noise and distractions fall back and the still, small voice is heard in our hearts, the language it speaks is pure and perfectly formed—in other words, sanskrita. The Sanskrit language that we find in dictionaries and learned works of grammar reflects this perfect universal language.

Sanskrit is ancient, yet it is as relevant today as it was thousands of years ago. That which is timeless is always relevant.

When I use the term "Sanskrit," I will usually be referring to the ancient language of Indian scripture and philosophy, taught in universities and chanted in āshrams. However, some seekers use "Sanskrit" to mean that limitless language of the Universe heard by those with "ears to hear"; that still small voice that is forever calling to all of us, telling us the beautiful limitless truth of who we really are. This form of Sanskrit, this "voice," is what aspirants at the higher levels of conscious spiritual development hear. Later in this book I will deal with the seven gateways to transformation that a seeker passes through to attain these higher levels of conscious development.

Delving Deeper into Sanskrit Language and Meaning

Sanskrit is one of the root languages in the extensive Indo-European linguistic family. This family of languages includes Hindi and Gujarati, but also Latin, Greek, German, French, Italian and English. Scholars consider Sanskrit to be "a mother of languages."

The Sanskrit vocabulary and grammatical system is extensive, scientific and precise. As a rule, Sanskrit words, even nouns, come from a verbal root (dhātu धातु). A verb is an action word, it is energy; something is happening. Thus, a verbal root for a word, is the energy behind the meaning. Sanskrit words therefore, are related to some form of energy or action.

For example, take the word "jñāna" (ज्ञान), the Sanskrit word for "knowledge." This word means "knowing, becoming acquainted with knowledge, especially the Higher knowledge derived from meditation on the One Universal Spirit." This word is derived from the verbal root jñā (ज्ञा), which contains the energy of all forms of knowledge and knowing. Every word derived from jñā carries the full force of this universal energy. This energy even turns up in English. "Kno" in "knowledge," and "gni" in "cognition" are forms of this Sanskrit verbal root jñā.

By looking into the verbal root forms of the Sanskrit words for "confidence," we can discover the energies that make up true confidence. We can discover what is happening within when we feel connected and self-confident. It also tells us what we need to do, to develop and discover confidence within ourselves.

There is a system of deriving the meanings of these verbal roots, unique to Sanskrit, devised by the grammarian Pāṇini. This system gives us an experiential approach to the discovery of meaning. Let us now consider this system of Pāṇini.

Pāṇini—a Sanskrit Scholar (4th to 6th century BCE)

Pāṇini (पाणिनि) was one of the wisest of Sanskrit scholars. We don't know exactly when he lived but academics think it was sometime in the period between the 4th to 6th centuries BCE (Before the Common Era).

He left an ingenious method for discovering the inner meaning of Sanskrit words which takes us beyond dictionaries and other reference works. In this system, Pāṇini tells us where to look to discover that essential meaning of the root forms of words.

In the case of jñā, the verbal root of jñāna (knowledge), Pāṇini indicates that the activity of knowing something—knowledge—is found when we are engaged "in teaching, informing and instructing." So, the way to know something is to teach it, to pass it on to someone else. The *Taittirīya Upanishad* states that, "Learning and teaching are necessary," because this is what transforms mere information into knowledge.

The Power of Meaning: It Determines Our Reality

The meaning we give to something determines our reality and life experience. If you see a grizzly bear coming towards you, then the meaning, or interpretation, in that moment will be one of danger, fear and survival. If you see a kitten charging at you, the meaning and experience is different. For the most part, we are unconscious of the meanings we lay over our reality.

We project the meanings we hold in our heart and mind onto our lives. The "meaning" of something, our interpretation of it, determines our thoughts, words and actions. We will experience fear if that is the meaning we hold. This is true of anger, love, and other emotions as well.

The values, attitudes and the level of confidence with which we face the world essentially create our life for us. We can give our life greater meaning and purpose by deepening our conception of these values and attitudes, and our level of confidence. By going back to the unchanging source wisdom in Sanskrit, we can redefine, clarify and realize a purer and more powerful meaning for the essential elements of our life, such as these values, attitudes and confidence.

Take for example a value that many share: peace.

For many of us "peace" is a wonderful quality that we value highly. For most of us peace is that calmness and serenity that shows itself only when conflict and disharmony have been banished.

However, when we look at the Sanskrit word for "peace"—shānti (शान्ति)—it takes this beautiful concept and tells us that peace is experienced when we are tranquil, and when we see it everywhere, and when our own actions are peaceful. In other words, peace is present when we feel it within ourselves, and then look out and see it everywhere, even if the circumstances seem less than peaceful.

When we assimilate this deeper meaning, it redefines and clarifies our understanding of true peace. Our realization of this deeper meaning shows itself in our attitude and actions that naturally and easily become more peaceful. This is how we start to develop strong and deep roots within ourself and respond to the world effectively, compassionately and realistically.

Going back to the origins of meaning through Sanskrit in this way, is like pulling back the string of a bow. The further back the arrow is pulled on the string, the further and straighter the arrow travels towards its target. There is minimum effort, and maximum power and energy in the flight of the arrow.

Timeless Wisdom Traditions

The ancient and timeless wisdom traditions of East and West have provided humanity with an unbroken thread of connection to consciousness throughout the millennia. It is a thread of wisdom and knowledge. The purpose of this thread is to provide source wisdom, and to make it ever-available for people to follow, so they can always realize the truth of themselves.

> "The great householders of the past, men famous for their learning and wisdom, had this in mind when they said: 'Let no man say there is anything we have not heard, thought, seen.'
> They knew everything."
>
> —Shrī Purohit Swāmi and W. B. Yeats,
> *Chandogya Upanishad, The Ten Principal Upanishads*

In today's world this source wisdom is available with a casual Internet search, a browse through a book shop or a visit to your local library. Texts that were kept exclusively for sages, priests, teachers and their students, are now there for the asking. The knowledge was carefully protected, and if a person desired this wisdom, they had to leave their worldly life, and study with these teachers behind closed doors. For centuries this wisdom was secret, now it's readily accessible.

British scholars such as Sir William Jones in India in the late 1800s, took some time to coax the knowledge of the sacred texts and Sanskrit from the priestly Brahmin sages. He and others began to translate some of the Sanskrit texts which contained profound wisdom previously unheard of. From there, English-language speakers began to discover this timeless wisdom. The American philosopher Emerson kept a much-valued copy of the *Bhagavad Gītā*. In the Royal College of Music, there is a precious manuscript page upon which Beethoven had copied out various verses and passages from the sacred texts of the *Upanishads*.

Yet, despite this smorgasbord of wisdom and knowledge now so easily available in shops, libraries, online, social media, printed on coffee mugs, desk calendars and fridge magnets, there are record rates of anxiety disorders, stress, unhappiness and a lack of fulfillment. The timeless wisdom traditions which offer solutions to all of these problems are available but are not being availed. The missing link is practice. To hear what this source wisdom is saying is one thing, to put it into practice is quite another.

Practice

There is no change without practicing. By practicing we transform. Practice is like exercising a muscle; it increases in strength with appropriate training. We become good at whatever we practice.

In fact, we are practicing all the time, we are always practicing something: a thought, a feeling, a word, an action.

The question is: What are we practicing?

If we practice thinking the same things, feeling the same things and doing the same things, then we can expect to get the same outcomes and experiences.

When we consciously choose to try something new to increase our awareness and improve our well-being, we can be sure that our experience will change.

All the practices in this book, if tried conscientiously, will lead to change and to the establishment of Conscious Confidence. You will find three levels of practices to use: starter, intermediate, and advanced. You might start simply with one practice at a level that feels comfortable for you. The important thing is to start practicing each day.

The practices are aimed at providing you with plenty of choices for how you can apply this knowledge directly in your daily life. You won't know if it works until you experience it. Just select one of the practices that piques your curiosity. Try it for a day or a week.

There are three "time" factors to practicing, all of which are necessary. They are: Frequency, Duration and Extent. Frequency is how often you practice. Duration is how long you practice for, and Extent is the period of time have you been practicing – a day, a week, a month, or years. For example:

- Frequency: How often do you meditate? – Once a day
- Duration: How long do you meditate for? – 20 minutes
- Extent: How long have you been meditating for? – 20 years

Tools for Achieving Timeless Wisdom

Our most valuable equipment to work with as we seek to attain timeless wisdom is our faculties, our energy, our capacity to apply intelligence and effort. We have a physical body, which moves us through the world and is always anchored in the present moment. We also have faculties beyond the physical. We have the vast, powerful and fine inner instrument of our mind and our heart.

In the Sanskrit wisdom tradition there are four aspects to the mind and heart:

- Manas (मनम्): The Thinking Mind aka "the Monkey Mind"
- Buddhi (बुद्धि): The Intellect or Intelligence
- Chitta (चित्त): Deep Memory aka the Heart
- Aham (अहम्): The Limitless Sense of Existence,
  or Ahamkāra (अहंकार): The Limited Sense of Existence

Let's look at each part in turn.

Manas: The Thinking Mind

Manas is the interpretive function of the mind. What does it interpret? The sense impressions: all sounds, touch, sights, tastes and smells. The impressions are neutral, and they are being received constantly. Because Manas only deals in sense impressions, these can only be after something has been experienced. The impressions are always from the past. Much like pulling out files from a drawer, Manas pulls from our sense memories to interpret new experiences.

Manas has the power of speech. Manas is what chats away in our head and comments on everything all day long. Manas is the thinking part of the mind that constantly proposes, and counter-proposes, presents one thing after another, makes simple associations until it weaves a web of thoughts circling around. Manas is confident in one moment and full of doubt the next, it craves certainty but can never find it. It can be easily distracted.

This function of mind is often referred to as "The Monkey Mind." In Hinduism it is personified as Indra, in Greek mythology as Hermes, in Roman mythology as Mercury and in Shakespeare as Puck in *A Midsummer Night's Dream*.

Buddhi: The Intellect or Intelligence

The next faculty of the mind, the Buddhi or the Intellect, shines brightly with the light of intelligence. It is with this light that the Buddhi discerns truth from untruth, the real from the unreal. This is the power of Reason.

The Intellect, if we use it properly, supervises the active thinking "Monkey Mind." It evaluates what is presented by Manas. It is the seat of genuine creativity, for it is from here that something new can come forth, as the Intellect can encompass the past, present and future. Manas, the active thinking mind, can only present experiences from the past. Take for example a meeting called to decide some course of action, such as a board meeting at a company or a staff meeting at a school. If the participants engage their intellect then the events that led up to the present situation can be identified clearly, the various proposals for moving forward can be assessed accurately, and the eventual decision and plan of action can be made to achieve the best outcome.

Chitta: Deep Memory or the Heart

The Chitta is a storehouse of memories. It holds the memory of who we are. This memory goes beyond the roles we play in our life and our personality. It is the memory of the pure consciousness which is at the heart of who we truly are.

The nature of the Chitta is like a crystal-clear lake. It can reflect anything perfectly, absolutely anything. If it is still, like calm still water, the reflection is perfect and clear. However, if it is disturbed and churned up by our reaction to life's challenges and triumphs, then the reflection is distorted and unclear. So, when we are calm, we can remember who we are in truth, and when we are agitated, we can't remember. Unsteady emotions render the reflection unclear.

Calm, steady, strong and positive attitudes and emotions allow the reflection and memory to function naturally, so we view our life clearly and in perspective.

Aham or Ahamkāra: the feeling of existence, either limitless (aham) or limited (ahamkāra)

Aham is a sense or "feeling" of existence. This is the limitless feeling or self-awareness that we are here now, "I Am." It's a pure and simple feeling. This feeling of existence is utterly present, and yet deeply peaceful and satisfying. It encompasses everything, it is one and undivided. It is this feeling of existence which unites us all.

Ahamkāra, the limited feeling of existence, is a compound of aham + kāra. Aham, "I Am", is pure being with no beginning and no end. It is universal and unmixed with any identification with experiences. With ahamkāra however, we do not say "I Am" but "I am (something)." Kāra means "an act or action or any created thing"; it is the "something" that follows "I am." For example: I am stupid, I am clever, I am ugly, I am beautiful, I am poor, I am rich, I am smarter than you, I am a lawyer, I am a mother, I am a father, I am walking, I am sitting. The list is endless!

These additions to "aham" are not in themselves inherently good or bad. They are temporary states we experience as we move through our life in the physical world. They have no independent existence. They need the consciousness of aham—I am - to exist. Aham itself is unchanged and unaffected by the addition of these actions and roles. The person who is awake and conscious, picks up these actions and roles, and when they are no longer needed puts them down again.

However, adding "kāra" to "aham" means that we experience a limit on our feeling of existence. These limits can come to define us. We become identified with these roles. We can come to believe that we are a lawyer, a teacher, a mother, and forget that we are, in truth, limitless consciousness, playing a role. This is not to diminish the importance of fulfilling these roles skillfully and beautifully. However, the identification with the role, whatever it is, can become narrow and turn into a feeling that we are small, weak and lacking in confidence.

31

The key is to be conscious, awake and aware. Manas weaves all this identification quite naturally. If we are unaware of it, we will unconsciously believe these transitory ideas and feel that we are limited and small. This simply isn't the case. This is why we need the proper foundations of timeless wisdom and knowledge to remind us of who we really are, and the transformative power of practice, to restore the natural functions of this powerful and fine inner instrument of mind and heart.

The story of The Monkey and the Bamboo Pole illustrates how we can deal with Manas, or the monkey mind we all have.

— ♦ —

The Monkey and the Bamboo Pole

Once there was a man who desired to spend his time in deep meditation and prayer. He wanted to realize the universal truth of himself. He was a farmer and householder, so he had many responsibilities and tasks to perform every day. This took up most of his time, and he knew that ignoring them was not the way to peace and fulfillment either.

♦

One day a monkey turned up on his doorstep. The monkey was a tricky character who could appear very attractive in one moment, but like a monster in the next. He made an offer to the farmer:

"I'm here to help you. I will do absolutely anything you instruct me to do."

The farmer was delighted. This was the answer to his prayers for help.

"There is one catch to this arrangement," the monkey said.

"Yes, yes, please tell me," the farmer replied.

"You must keep me fully occupied for every second of every day. There can't be a moment that I'm not fully engaged with something to do. If I'm idle for even a moment, I will immediately create havoc, and this will eventually kill you," the monkey explained.

The farmer agreed to this arrangement.

◆

The farmer began by giving the monkey his first job. The monkey disappeared, and was back in a moment, with the task fully completed. So, the farmer gave him the next task, and this too was done in an instant. The farmer gave him another, and yet another thing to do around the farm and in the house. All the jobs were done perfectly and with amazing efficiency.

So, each and every day, the farmer would spend his days giving task after task to the monkey to complete, knowing that he had to be ready with another job in order to prevent the monkey from creating the havoc which would eventually kill the farmer. The problem the farmer now had was he still couldn't meditate and pray, because he had to keep the monkey constantly occupied. Occupying the monkey became the farmer's new job!

◆

Finally, the farmer came up with a solution.

He instructed the monkey, "Go to the woods and cut down a ten-foot length of bamboo."

The monkey disappeared and was back in a moment with the bamboo just as he had been told.

"Now clean it up, so the pole is smooth and perfectly prepared."

The monkey again set to work, and in the blink of an eye, had created a beautiful ten-foot bamboo pole.

"Now set it firmly in the ground so it stands upright without moving."

Again, this was done in a flash.

◆

"From now on, unless I give you a specific task to perform around the farm or in the house, you are to climb up and down this bamboo pole without stopping in between times."

The monkey followed these instructions to the letter for many weeks. He performed all his designated tasks about the place, and in between jobs, he climbed up and down the ten-foot bamboo pole without stopping. This kept the monkey fully occupied all the time. He couldn't create havoc, which eventually would kill his master. The farmer was very happy, because now he could spend most of his time in meditation and prayer, which was his heart's desire, without all his worldly responsibilities being ignored.

After several weeks, the monkey was exhausted.

◆

He went to his master and said, "I give up. I shall be very happy to perform all necessary tasks in service to you. In between times, I will sit quietly by your side and wait for you to give me something to do. I promise I will not create havoc that will eventually kill you. You are safe."

—◆—

This is a traditional story that has been used to teach humanity for ages. What can we learn from it?

The tricky monkey stands for the Manas—the active thinking mind.

The farmer is the Buddhi—the Intellect, Reason and Intelligence.

The bamboo pole is mental discipline such as speaking an affirmation of truth, repeating a mantra (a word we focus on and say in our minds over and over again), or simply giving single-pointed and undistracted attention to a task in hand.

The point of the story is that the active mind must be kept fully occupied all the time; otherwise, it will immediately begin to weave a web of trouble and havoc.

Once the mind is sufficiently disciplined through proper practice, it surrenders and will be still and quiet; waiting patiently and ready to complete any task given to it. A disciplined mind is a truly amazing instrument—efficient, capable and willing to serve.

The story illustrates the essential need for regular and frequent simple daily practice.

Finding Sanskrit Everywhere

Sanskrit can turn up anywhere. You can find it in a bookshop, on TV or you can find it when ordering some tea.

A few years ago, my husband and I were in Kansas City, and we went into a café for tea. A young woman behind the counter took our order. I noticed some Sanskrit words tattooed up her arm. The devanāgarī lettering was beautifully done. We commented upon the tattoo, which was one of the great sayings of Indian wisdom, "Thou Art That" तत्त्वमसि (tattvamasi). We read it aloud for her because she didn't know what it said. She also couldn't remember what it meant, so we told her. She just liked the look of it and felt good having something of significance that held deep and profound meaning.

On another occasion back in Australia, a young man working as a waiter in a café served us our lunch one day. He had a small Sanskrit tattoo on his wrist. I asked him about it: "That's a beautiful-looking Sanskrit tattoo, what does it say?" He smiled and looked pleased, he touched it with great affection for it clearly meant a great deal to him. He wasn't very clear on its meaning, he thought it meant something to do with "service." The tattoo said: सेव (seva), which means "selfless service." We read it together and had a brief, meaningful conversation about the significance of service in our lives.

A few months ago, while we were travelling in Australia, we met another lady behind a reception desk who had a tattoo up her inner arm: ॐ प्रेम सर्वान् जयति (OM prema sarvān jayati). She knew the meaning of her tattoo: OM Love Conquers All. It was very significant for her. Her face lit up when we remarked upon it. She was delighted that someone could read it and also knew what it meant.

Discovering Deeper Meanings

One area of Sanskrit that was integral to my practical philosophy studies, was to research the detailed and deeper meanings of individual Sanskrit words. We did this before meditating and reflecting on statements in Sanskrit from the wisdom traditions such as the *Upanishads* or the *Bhagavad Gītā*.

Why did we go back to the Sanskrit meanings?

Because all impressions are filtered through our thoughts and belief systems, which are, for the most part, limited in nature and based on the past. This filtering is unconscious, and colours the meaning we give to everything. One effective way of overcoming this filtering is to go back to the Sanskrit etymology. It puts those unconscious meanings under the spotlight.

In this focused study, I experienced many "Ah-ha" moments, where the deeper and more profound Sanskrit derivations for a particular word highlighted a limited view I had of its meaning.

One example was with the word "sarva" (सर्व). It is a very common word, which turns up a lot in spiritual texts, and it means "all." I had researched "sarva" many times before, so I thought I knew what it meant: all, nothing more.

On this occasion, I was tempted to skip over researching "sarva" yet again. However, as a matter of discipline, I focused on the word as if for the first time. I looked up "sarva" in the Sanskrit to English dictionary and read with full attention, letting go of any of my assumptions. This little word has a very full list of meanings in the dictionary.

Through this simple discipline of remaining open, and much to my surprise, I connected with this word in a profound way. I experienced understanding that was not merely an intellectual appreciation. I realized in direct experience that the true meaning of "all"—sarva—is not just "a lot," but everything. It includes everything down to the tiniest atom, and up to the universe and beyond. There is nothing that isn't included in sarva. When the Sanskrit wisdom texts refer to "all," they really mean "all"; nothing is left out.

I also realized that I typically place limits around "all" so that it is reduced to meaning merely "a lot." This was a revelation, a flash of insight which highlighted a limited meaning, and expanded my understanding. I set aside "my way" and stuck to a discipline and gave full attention.

This is a simple example of the power of Sanskrit to uncover old concepts and preconceived notions which limit our view and therefore our experience of life and of ourselves. This can lead to imbalance in our lives. Our emotions don't align with our thoughts, and our actions don't match either of these. In the next chapter we look at this misalignment and how to get back into balance.

Chapter Two

Balancing the Body, Mind, and Heart

"Self rides in the chariot of the body, intellect the firm-footed charioteer, discursive mind the reins. Senses are the horses, objects of desire the roads. When Self is joined to body, mind, sense, none but He enjoys.

When a man lacks steadiness, unable to control his mind, his senses are unmanageable horses. But if he controls his mind, a steady man, they are manageable horses.

He who calls intellect to manage the reins of his mind reaches the end of his journey, finds there all-pervading Spirit."

—Shrī Purohit Swāmi and W. B. Yeats,
Katha Upanishad, The Ten Principal Upanishads

Now that we have a better understanding of the power of Sanskrit to guide us to deeper levels of meaning, we are ready to discover what happens when the body, mind, and heart are in alignment. When we are aligned, we feel strong, capable and confident. We find we have clarity and certainty, and our endeavors meet with success. For example, we know we need to get into shape, so we set a goal to exercise regularly. We're excited and resolved to follow through and we establish and stick to a weekly program. After three months, we feel healthier, happier and more energized. The alignment of our thoughts, feelings and actions increased our confidence, so that we will carry this forward and achieve even bigger fitness goals.

When we are out of alignment, it is much more difficult to attain clarity, certainty and success. We feel one way but act another. For example, a friend asks us for help; we agree, but we don't attend to it and it plays on our mind. It sours the relationship; eventually, we begin to avoid this friend.

The following story of the old farmer who said, "Well, let's just see how things turn out," illustrates what happens when body, mind, and heart are in alignment: We achieve equanimity.

━ ✦ ━

Well, Let's Just See How Things Turn Out

Once there was an old farmer who had an old horse. The horse looked tired, thin and weak. The farmer wanted to let the old horse live out the rest of its life with ease. So, he let the horse go free to roam around the hills and mountains.

The farmer's kind neighbours came to visit him and expressed their sadness that the farmer didn't have the horse to help with his farm work. They asked him, "Oh dear, you poor thing, what are you going to do around the farm without your horse to help?" The farmer replied calmly, "Well, let's just see how things turn out."

✦

Sometime later, the horse came back to the farm of its own accord. It was now healthy and strong after wandering the hills and eating all the fresh wild grasses. Ten new healthy younger horses also followed the older horse back into the stables. The neighbours excitedly gathered at the farm when they heard that the horse had returned. "Congratulations old farmer, you must be thrilled! Now you have all these horses that can work around the farm!" Once again, the farmer replied calmly, "Well, let's just see how things turn out."

✦

A few days later, the farmer's son was out with the new horses. They were still rather wild and needed training so that they could be of use with the farm work. As he rode one of the wild horses, it reared up and threw him off. He fell to the ground and couldn't walk because his leg was broken.

The neighbours came around and commiserated with the farmer that this was such bad luck. "This is terrible for you, we are so sorry. How will you manage to do all the farm work without your son's help?" The farmer thanked them for their concern but quietly said, "Well, let's just see how things turn out."

♦

A week later, a terrible war broke out. All the young men were called to fight in the army. The General's men came around the villages to conscript all the able-bodied men. The farmer's son was still recovering from his accident and was unable to walk. So, the General's men decided that the farmer's son was unfit to fight.

The farmer's neighbours came to visit and exclaimed to him, "How lucky is this, that your son hasn't been enlisted. You must be so glad! All our sons have been marched off to fight." The farmer, once more, calmly replied, "Well, let's just see how things turn out."

♦

The farmer worked steadily on the farm by himself while his son's leg healed. Once he had recovered and could return to work, he was left with a slight limp as he walked. The neighbours came around and said, "It's such a shame that your son can't walk properly. You must feel so bad about this." The farmer simply replied, "Well, let's just see how things turn out."

♦

After months of battle, many young men of the villages were killed whilst fighting. The old farmer and his son were the most able-bodied farmers left once the war was over. They worked hard and became rich. They generously helped all their neighbours, and even other villages in the area. The neighbours said, "You're so kind and generous, and we're very fortunate. You must be so very happy!" To this the farmer softly replied, "Well, let's just see how things turn out."

It is difficult to sustain a sense of balance and calm in the face of changing and sometimes challenging events. Seeing the bigger picture is one way of finding a point of steadiness in the ups and downs of life and aligning body, mind, heart and spirit.

You are not being encouraged to settle for passivity or a lack of feeling but rather a detachment from the highs and lows of emotions you associate with events and circumstances.

Prioritizing can help you maintain balance in your life, as the following story illustrates.

—◆—

Filling the Jar

A teacher stood in front of his class one day. He carefully placed an empty glass jar on the desk. He then took out a bag of large rocks and filled the jar to the top.

He turned to the class and asked, "Is this jar full?"

The students immediately agreed that, yes, the jar was full.

The teacher then got out a bag of smaller pebbles and proceeded to fill the jar further. He gave the jar a shake to let the smaller pebbles fall down in between the larger rocks. He then asked again, "Is the jar completely full now?"

The students agreed that the jar was completely full now.

The teacher then continued to fill the jar right to the top with sand. He poured the sand so it filled up any remaining space. The students all agreed that the jar was now really full.

The teacher gave the students time to reflect on the point of his demonstration. He eventually explained what this was about.

◆

"The jar stands for a person's life. The larger rocks represent the important things in our life. Things such as family, loved ones, close friends, health and well-being.

"Without the smaller pebbles and sand filling up space in our life, our life would still be full and meaningful. The larger rocks stand for things that are of primary importance in our life.

"The smaller pebbles represent our job, house, hobbies, and interests. There's still enough space in our life for these, but they are not the primary source of fulfillment. These things are more transitory and of secondary importance.

"Finally, the sand stands for all the material things and small tasks and errands in our life. This includes watching television, time on social media and spending time acquiring possessions. None of these are actually essential, and usually are a way of whiling away time.

◆

"The key point is that in order to live a happy, balanced, healthy and successful life in all areas, you need to get your priorities right. If you fill up your life first with all the small things, like filling the empty jar with sand first, then there won't be any space for the important things. Your life will be filled with unimportant and insignificant things. Start by filling your life with the essential and important things first, and there will always be room for the other things around that.

◆

"Give due attention first to health, exercise, well-being, family, loved ones and goals. This means that your daily 'to do' list of errands, schedules and diaries won't rule your life and fill up your days."

"So, what rocks will you fill your day with tomorrow?"

These two stories teach us about two essential elements of staying balanced and in alignment: equanimity and priorities. Many of us enjoy the drama of soaring high on excitement, only to be brought down later with disappointment. We're addicted to the rush of the roller-coaster ride each day, no matter how exhausting it can be. We might say we want balance and equanimity, but our thoughts are out of alignment with our actions. On some level, we crave the excitement.

Do you overvalue excitement? And do you underestimate the value of balance?

What Does Sanskrit Teach Us about Balance?

The Sanskrit word for balance is "santulana."

"Santulana" (संतुलन), to weigh one thing against another or to balance together.

The root for this Sanskrit word meaning "balance" is "tul" (तुल्). This root means "weighing and determining the weight of something by lifting it up."

Pāṇini's statement for this root "tul" is: "That measuring is to be found in the act of measuring." This seems rather circular and obvious, so how does this help our understanding?

The key point of this word "balance" is measuring. Measuring means knowing when to stop one activity before embarking on the next. An analogy may help, so imagine a set of scales. If we intend to measure out a quantity of sand, and we want to keep the scales balanced, then we need to measure out the same quantity on each side.

First, we pour an amount of sand into one side.

Clearly the scales will be unbalanced at this point because there's nothing on the other side to counter-balance yet. Then we start carefully pouring sand into the other side. Slowly both sides of the scales move closer to being level and balanced.

Now we reach the crucial moment, where we determine that both sides of the scales are balanced, and we stop pouring. If we continue to pour more sand, we will create another imbalance on the other side.

Achieving balance hinges on stopping at the right moment.

Thus, the essence of balance and measure is knowing when to stop. This can be obvious such as when we work too long and too hard and it is time to go home to our family and rest. On another level, it can be time to stop thinking and to take action, or it can be time to get our feelings under control and begin to reflect on the lesson we can learn from a challenging experience. Too much thought and not enough emotion causes an imbalance and we can be cold and disconnected. If we are overly emotional, we can be irrational and unsteady. When we are not aligned, our actions and choices do not balance our head and our heart, and the body usually bears the brunt through stress, tension and a lack of well-being.

Aligning the Aspects of Ourselves, Becoming a Whole Person

Many of the timeless wisdom traditions describe in various ways how a human being is comprised of different aspects. The *Katha Upanishad*, for example, uses the analogy of the chariot and charioteer. It likens the physical body to a chariot, the senses to the horses, the active, chattering, thinking mind to the reins, and the steady intellect to the "firm-footed" charioteer. The objects that we desire are the roads.

When we lack steadiness and the active mind is discursive and distracted, then our senses are like unmanageable horses. We chase our desires and are ruled by feelings and passing thoughts. The poor old body is forced to go along for the ride. This lack of balance and alignment is all too common.

In Book Nine of Plato's *Republic*, the ancient Greek philosopher Socrates gives us another model. He says we are divided into four parts which he calls Appetite (described as a many-headed beast), Passion (described as a lion) and Reason. The fourth element is created when these three combine to make the Whole Man. Misalignment takes place when either Appetite or Passion rule. Balance is achieved when Reason is in the driver's seat.

Some think that the body, mind, and heart constitute who we are. However, spirit is the fourth aspect of ourselves. These aspects can also be described as four different bodies: a physical body, a mental body, an emotional body and a spiritual body. These four bodies can be conceived to be like Russian dolls, one nesting inside the other. All four bodies make up the whole person and need to be in alignment and balanced if we are to experience happiness, wellness, and fulfillment.

Each of these bodies—even the spiritual body—requires food (or nourishment), exercise and rest. Food, or nourishment, can be seen as what is taken in, exercise as what is given out, and rest is a state of inactivity and repose which allows for restoration and refreshment.

Food, Exercise, and Rest for Balance

We all know we need to provide the physical body with the right amount of appropriate food, exercise and rest for it to remain healthy, strong, balanced and energized: not too much of anything, and not too little. In an ideal world we would ensure regular fresh, balanced and nourishing meals. Daily movement and deep breathing of suitable intensity comprise exercise, and sufficient good quality sleep for rest. All this varies according to age, the seasons and what we're doing at the time. We naturally adjust what and how much we eat according to how we feel. We exercise according to our energy levels, the weather and what we enjoy. If we're tired, we have more rest. Despite changing circumstances, our aim is the same: to have a healthy body and to feel good.

Appropriate food, exercise and rest also helps the mental, emotional, and spiritual bodies to experience balance. As a result, we feel integrated, whole and aligned, which is our natural state. A continuous state of stress, fear and weakness is unnatural.

Balancing the Mind or Mental Body

What is appropriate food, exercise and rest for the mind to ensure that it is clear, quiet, efficient and creative? Food for the mind consists of relaxing study of interesting, substantial stimulating knowledge and wisdom. This could be reading good quality uplifting literature or listening to beautiful music and sounds.

Exercise for the mind can be problem solving, critical thinking and discussion where our assumptions, habitual attitudes and beliefs are challenged, and we have to think more deeply. It can also be learning something new and demanding such as how to speak a foreign language, play a musical instrument or learn a specific type of dance that you have never done before.

Choosing positive thoughts and life-affirming attitudes is also excellent exercise for the mind. (You will learn more about this later.)

The mind needs to be nourished and exercised by requiring it to discern what is finer and better from what is coarse and unedifying. We do this with our food and exercise for the body, and it is the same for mental food and exercise for the mind.

Rest for the mind is essential, and the most direct way is through meditation or giving full attention to a task. Let the mind rest with something enjoyable, and not too challenging, such as drawing, painting, playing a musical instrument or quiet reading and contemplation. By doing this and not allowing it to be distracted by every passing thought that drifts by, is a key method of giving the mind some rest and refreshment.

Meditation itself is often called the "master key" because it feeds all the bodies and gives rest at every level. Sometimes, it can even be a form of exercise when mental activity clouds the process. There are many ways to meditate just as there are many ways to get food, exercise, and rest for your four bodies. Find a way that works for you.

Mental rest can come from exercise that also strengthens the physical body. The four bodies are integrated, so what you find to be food for the mind can be food for the emotions, what you find restful for the body can also be restful for the emotions and the mind, and so on.

Balancing the Emotional Body

We nourish the heart with appropriate food when we experience beauty and magnificence, and emotions such as awe and wonder. Love, values and virtues are prime sources of food for the emotional body. Art, music, dance and creativity are also ways we feed the emotional body. Good company, deep friendships and connection provide our heart with the nourishment it needs so it can be happy, loving, steady, and resilient. Being out in nature and appreciating its beauty and variety uplift and fill our emotional center with good food.

Consider how satisfied you can feel after a peaceful walk in a beautiful place. It's like having a delicious meal for the emotional body. Also, the mind can settle and rest when the emotions are well cared for, so this is how we start to come into alignment and balance.

We exercise the emotional body by being good company for others, and by practicing values and virtues each day. Engaging in the creative arts such as making beautiful music, art or dance are other excellent ways to exercise the emotional body.

Deep stillness in meditation, a peaceful walk, quiet contemplation of natural beauty, gazing at the stars, remaining still in the present moment and letting go of past and future narratives, all these are restful for the emotional body.

Having covered the body, the mind, and the heart and their need for nourishment, exercise and rest, we now come to the most important and powerful center of all. This is the seat of consciousness within us. It is who we truly are. The spiritual body is the lynchpin. If it receives everything it needs, then our life reflects this healthful condition by being aligned and balanced.

Balancing the Spiritual Body

Meditation is food for the spiritual body, along with prayer and keeping company with the words of the wise. All of these activities will help you feel a sense of connection, peace, and freedom.

Exercise for the spiritual body comes from seeing the best in everyone and every situation, listening to others fully with great care and openness, and giving full attention in the present moment to whatever is before us. Asking yourself important questions is also excellent exercise for the spirit. Questions such as, "Am I aware of myself now?" and "What is of highest importance to me now?"

Rest for the spiritual body comes again from meditation, and also journaling, prayer and mindfulness practice. Anytime we are inwardly calm and still is rest for the spiritual body.

Methods for Helping the Four Bodies Achieve Balance

Body	Food	Exercise	Rest
Physical	Fresh, nutritious food	Gym; sport; yoga; walking	Sleep; relaxation
Mental	Interesting, useful, stimulating subjects	Problem solving; discussion, debate; learning something new	Focused attention; restful mental activities
Emotional	Objects of beauty; nature; harmony; service to others	Creativity; singing; painting; drawing; music; service to others	Love; affection; tranquility; giving and receiving; meditation
Spiritual	Spiritual works; scripture; wisdom	Disciplined practices; prayer; overcoming limitations	Meditation; awareness

Recognizing Imbalances

We feel unbalanced and lacking in energy when we over- or under-eat, and when we eat food that doesn't suit our body. Also, when we exercise too much or too little, and sleep poorly or for too long. It can be an effort to get through the day doing simple tasks.

When we over-think an issue unproductively and repetitively, we are using the mind in a way that uses a lot of energy and brings no useful result. Typically, this type of thinking is negative, and is a recipe for tiring the mind as it is working without any proper food and rest. It's like chewing the same mouthful of food until there's nothing left in our mouth, but we keep chewing anyway.

The other type of mental activity which brings about imbalance is allowing the mind to present a loosely related stream of useless and negative thoughts. When our thinking jumps around from one random thought to another, we are using our mental energy in unproductive activity which has a deleterious effect on the physical, emotional and spiritual bodies. Sometimes this form of thinking can be part of the creative process, but often it leads nowhere, or it can spiral down into negativity. The easy test is to see if anything creative actually emerges from the process. If not, then stop.

When we hold on to the emotional charge of a past event or future projection, such as regretting something that happened yesterday or worrying about something that will happen tomorrow, we ride the inevitable cycle of highs and lows that these stories bring. We take a ride on an emotional roller-coaster that expends huge amounts of energy without any productive outcome. It is a very effective way of depleting our energy and leaves us susceptible and lacking resilience.

When we think one thing, feel another thing, say something different again, and then do yet another thing, we perpetuate a lack of connection to our values and what's important to us. This is how we remain disconnected with our spiritual body and who we really are.

The Choice to Rebalance and Get Back into Alignment

With knowledge from the wisdom traditions, we can make wiser choices that can help us get back into alignment. We know how good being in balance makes us feel—clearer, stronger, and calmer—but we live busy lives. Getting a proper balance of food, exercise and rest for each of the four bodies can be a challenge.

Wise choices are all about knowing when to stop one thing and start something else that is preferable or a higher priority right now. What may have been useful an hour ago becomes useless when it's time to stop. For example, overeating, no matter how healthy the food is, becomes unhealthy and causes imbalance. Sitting at your computer working on a project for too long can cause back and neck issues simply because you didn't stop for a break to stand up, stretch and walk around the room. Another example is over-analyzing an issue until you can't decide what to do and you won't take action.

Being connected, aligned and balanced is a natural state. The way to maintain alignment and balance, so we are connected, powerful, strong, happy and fulfilled is to know when to stop one thing and do something else. Not too much and not too little. Remember, the essence of measure and balance is knowing when to stop.

To provide appropriate daily food, exercise and rest for the whole person, and know when to stop one activity and move on to another requires presence, wisdom and discriminating choices. With practice (and you will soon learn some practices you can use), this becomes a natural, enriching and stress-free way to live and thrive.

I was working on my next radio show on my laptop in a local café in Sydney. Sitting at a table with her back towards me was a lovely young woman wearing headphones, working on her laptop. Her phone and a cup of coffee were next to her. I noticed that she had a Sanskrit tattoo on her arm. It was a single word. My curiosity was piqued, as I didn't recognize the word. So, I introduced myself and asked if I could look more closely at her Sanskrit tattoo. She graciously let me peer closely with my glasses!

The word was "santulana" (संतुलन).

I asked her the meaning, and she didn't really know, but she had been told it meant "balance." She just loved the beautiful shapes of the lettering and liked the idea of "balance" because that was what she needed in her life at the time. We discussed the meaning of "balance" and this was her definition: having the space and time for friends, family and herself as well as work commitments. That requires prioritizing and making choices about how to spend the hours of the day.

The One–Three–Nine Way to Achieve Balance

A teaching colleague of mine was studying the same system of philosophy, meditation, Sanskrit and traditional spiritual wisdom as I. We had been introduced to a simple principle of a daily balance of measured activities: each day is measured by one, three and nine.

- One hour of meditation per day; split into two half-hour periods, one in the morning and one in the evening, the ideal times being sunrise and sunset.
- Three hours of restful mental activity. This period of time needn't just be a single block of time each day, but a total of three hours per day. Restful activity could be, for example, study, or artistic, craft or creative pursuits, or quiet activities such as walking, tai-chi, yoga etc. The purpose is to spend three hours a day engaged in restful activity for the mind.
- Nine hours of work—such as your job or your business.

There are eleven hours unaccounted for in this one—three—nine measure. The remaining eleven hours are for all the basic necessities of life such as sleep, eating, bathing and housework.

My colleague, a brilliant man, was not one to take on anything from blind faith. He always assiduously tested everything and discovered for himself if a principle worked or didn't. His example of the practical application of something with reason and intelligence was of great importance to me, and I learnt so much from his approach.

On this occasion, he decided that he would use a period of two months to apply this daily one—three—nine measure to see if it worked. He was a man of natural discipline, so he was able to apply himself diligently, and follow the principle.

So, each day he meditated for a full thirty minutes in the morning and evening. He studied a number of subjects in which he had an interest and wanted to learn more. He also engaged in artistic pursuits such as painting and drawing, story writing and exercised by swimming and doing other enjoyable activities. He easily filled-up three hours every day with this range of restful and enjoyable activities.

Then he spent nine hours on his work, which was teaching at the time. So there was much to do each day in that career. He also made sure he stopped after nine hours and didn't do any more! The other eleven hours were occupied in the practical tasks of life, including sleep.

What was the outcome of this two-month experiment?

He enthusiastically reported that it was excellent; highly recommended. He felt happy, rested, calm and balanced. Like the farmer in the story, he didn't waste energy on things that hadn't yet happened. He was inspired by his studies, and the amount of time available each day was the thing that surprised him the most—he found there was plenty of it! He realized how much time each day is frittered away in distraction and avoidance. He delighted in how naturally productive he had been. It felt really good.

He also discovered he was far more efficient with practical jobs such as cleaning, laundry and bathing. He noticed how he was more conscious of what and how much he ate, and he slept naturally and awoke each morning well rested.

He had done a huge number of things over the two-month period, was inspired to continue, and by no means felt exhausted and depleted —quite the opposite.

One of the key lessons was stopping each activity at the right moment. This prioritizing is very much like the message in the story of filling the jar with rocks and sand. He had to be awake and aware for that. No matter how good something is, even meditation, there is a point to stop and move onto something else. He discovered that providing the body, mind, heart and spirit with appropriate food, exercise and rest each day connected him to a natural flow in life. He realized through his own direct experience that alignment and balance through measure is natural. It needn't be left for special occasions!

The exercises which follow, are all designed to allow you to achieve this level of balance, alignment, measure and harmony in your life. If followed carefully they will result in a feeling of energy, focus and add a sense of perspective to the many issues that press in on us and often create a feeling of overwhelm. It is a matter of creating space to come into alignment and balance.

Practices

Starter Discovering Your Own Daily Balance and Measure

If you are inspired to try the one—three—nine measure, then I encourage you to experiment like my colleague. Find what works for you. Perhaps explore working up to it.

- If you don't already have a system of meditation, find one that suits you. Try a little each day; five minutes or so each morning, then build up.

- Then incorporate into your day some study or reading of something uplifting, inspiring and interesting. Something that isn't "work." You may have wanted to do something for a long time but never gotten around to it. Now's your time; do a little every day for a week and see what that is like. Again, build up steadily to the full three-hour measure.

- Remember to include some physical exercise into the mix. It needn't be strenuous; something that allows the mind to rest while the body is moving, for example: walking, yoga, tai-chi, dance, swimming, cycling in a lovely environment. Include some creative things too. Pick up your violin that you used to learn as a child or sit down at the piano. Sketch a beautiful scene or draw your favorite pet. Why not try one of the colouring books for adults with beautiful designs and pictures which provide an easy and creative way to rest the mind. This isn't about becoming an expert or producing a perfect piece. It's about engaging in a restful activity for the body, mind and heart. In any case, the more frequently you do these activities, the better you will become at them quite naturally.

- Now see how daily meditation and time spent doing some restful mental activity affects your work. Are you more efficient and less stressed? Is work more enjoyable and satisfying? Are you a more productive and positive member of the team?

- Finally, are you feeling healthier and more rested? Are you naturally making better food choices? Do you find the desire for certain things fading? Can you spend a little more time each day unplugged from your devices and out of the virtual world?

Be watchful for any strict rules being imposed from within yourself, of how it's meant to be or what you're meant to do. Don't let the idea of "perfect" drive out "the good." Experiment and see for yourself what it's like in your own experience.

`Intermediate` Do As You Say

Alignment of thought, word and deed is integrity. This is a very powerful discipline.

- Find an area of your life where you are conscious of saying one thing and doing another. Become aware of this. The practice is to make a deliberate effort in this one area only, to align thought, word and deed. This is not an exercise in self-criticism, it is an opportunity to improve self-discipline—an essential element for success in life.

- For example, if you undertake to do something, then you align your thoughts, words and deeds, so you actually follow through and do what you said you would do. This could be as innocuous as saying to someone that you'll call them back, and then you don't do it. The reasons could be quite innocent such as you forgot, or something else came up and you did that first, and then time got away from you. If you said you would call someone back, then do whatever it takes to ensure that you will do just that—call them back.

    Simply find one thing where there is not alignment of your thought, your words, and your action, and resolve to follow through instead. This does require increased self-awareness.

- Another aspect of this practice is to be careful about promising to do things! One suggestion is to refrain from saying "Yes" immediately. You can say "Maybe," and later when you have had a bit of space to consider, you can decide whether it's "Yes" or "No."

This practice will raise your self-awareness considerably, because you will become very careful of what you say you will do. Your choice of thoughts and speech will become conscious, as your integrity clarifies and strengthens.

`Advanced` Higher Level Integrity

This is an advanced level exercise of aligning thought, word and deed. It takes the previous practice of "Do as You Say" to another level.

- First become aware of when you are criticizing someone or requiring them to do or say something differently. This could be a family member or a co-worker for example. If you are honest with yourself, you may find that you are guilty of the same behavior, which you have judged as unacceptable. You might not say anything directly to the person being criticized, but you might think it or say it to someone else. Behaviors you criticize in others might include interrupting a conversation, or regularly turning the conversation to themself.

- Now that you are aware of a specific behavior, consciously stop behaving that way yourself and surrender any requirement that the other person behave differently.

- It is best to work with a very specific identifiable behavior, so you can be focused and purposeful with this practice. This is exercising self-discipline and conscious choice at a powerful level.

There is a secret here. We usually criticize the failings in others which we recognize. We can only recognize what we know from our own behavior, otherwise we wouldn't recognize it! So, our judgements and criticisms of others deserve our gratitude, as they show us with alarming accuracy where to begin on ourselves.

Now that we have looked at the whole person and the alignment of body, mind, heart and spirit, we need to address the issue of waking up. Increased levels of awareness are a key element to making a move to Conscious Confidence. This is what we will cover in the next chapter.

Chapter Three

CONSCIOUS AND UNCONSCIOUS CONFIDENCE

"…This is a strange repose, to be asleep
With eyes wide open, standing, speaking, moving,
And yet so fast asleep."

—William Shakespeare,
The Tempest (Act 2, Scene 1)

Confidence is having inner strength, self-assurance, self-esteem and resilience. You may look at people who seem to be confident and wonder how they have achieved this. Are they just lucky and were born with it? Are they truly confident?

You may find your own confidence has no lasting foundation, and therefore evaporates when the conditions are not perfect. Does your confidence come and go just when you need it most?

There is a type of confidence that comes from habit and familiarity. For example: driving to work, cooking familiar meals without a recipe, brushing your teeth, social functions with well-known friends and family, performing familiar tasks at work. We can be good at these things and do them well. Confidence like this is based on repetition. We develop skills and know-how. Much of our "comfort zone" in our world is formed by this familiarity.

Good routines are important for our health. Regular food, exercise, recreation and sleep are essential. A healthy community and society depend on everyone playing their part to maintain stability and balance. Children need this as they grow up.

However, familiarity, routine and habit encourage minimal attention in the present. These are the conditions ripe for becoming unconscious, unaware and asleep. What happens when the circumstances change? Are we full of doubt? Do we feel threatened? Can we respond and take action? Do we become upset and agitated? Have we allowed our confidence to be dependent on familiar situations and actions? Can we adapt and thrive in changing situations? Can we take our confidence with us from the "familiar" to the new and the challenging?

We can if we have Conscious Confidence: confidence that is based in recognizing the opportunities inherent in the situations we find ourselves in, and also in recognizing the strength and power of our self. We are limitlessly free, but we often feel ourselves to be bound. It is limiting ideas, negative feelings and old habits based on a partial and inaccurate view of the world and of ourselves that binds us. Waking up to Conscious Confidence begins the process of going free.

The following story illustrates what happens when we do not see the truth of what we are experiencing.

— ◆ —

The Camel Driver

In a wealthy city lived a camel driver. He was the best camel driver in the city. His animals were hired by merchants to carry their wares to far-flung markets. One day the camel driver hired an apprentice.

He trained his new assistant in all the skills of his trade. The young apprentice learnt how to load the bundles, how to feed and water the camels, and how to find places of shade and rest along the trade routes.

The apprentice was eager to learn and very quickly acquired all the skills that the camel driver showed him.

◆

One day the camel driver, pleased with his apprentice, took him aside.

"My boy," he began, "I am impressed with your diligence and skill. Tell me, is there anything more about the business of camel driving that you want to know?"

The young man thought for a moment.

"Master," he said, "when we are on a journey and we stop for the night I see the other camel drivers and their men spending time securing their camels to posts and rails, driving stakes into the ground and tying their beasts to prevent them wandering off in the night. However, your camels merely sit at your command, you run your hand around their necks, and they remain where you have put them until the morning comes. What magic is it that you perform?"

The master laughed but said nothing.

A few days later he took his apprentice to the camel market. It was time to buy a new beast for their herd. They bought a fine looking camel and they led it home.

♦

The master took this camel, made it sit and then tied it carefully and securely with a rope. He then passed his hand around the camel's neck several times. He did this day after day, each time securely tying the new camel with rope, and then passing his hands around the neck.

One day he left the rope and merely mimed the action of tying, and then passing his hand around the camel's neck. The camel stayed where it was all night.

The apprentice understood.

"Master," he said, "this creature, although free, believes itself to be bound, and acts accordingly."

The master smiled and nodded at his apprentice.

The camel driver created the belief in the camels that they were tied up, so that all he needed to do was pass his hand around their neck. However, we do this to ourselves. Just as the camels believed that they were tied up with rope around their necks, we reinforce ideas such as: I am stupid, I can't do this, I don't have enough time, I'm not good enough...and the list goes on.

This story illustrates how we bind ourselves mentally. We are actually free; we have free choice at every moment. We can choose to be, do and have anything. However, we repeatedly hold a belief that we are more limited in our freedom than we actually are.

When we awaken to our potential, and to this process of limitation, then we can free ourselves. No one can do this for us. Being awake, aware and conscious is the key to seeing the ideas that form the limits and letting them go.

What Does Sanskrit Teach Us about Being Conscious?

The Sanskrit word for conscious is "chetana."

"Chetana" (चेतन), to be visible, sentient, intelligent, percipient, understanding, perceptive. Having sense, consciousness and insight. An intelligent being.

"Chetana" (being conscious), is derived from the root "chit" (चित्). This root means: to perceive, observe, attend to, understand, know, comprehend and take notice of. The Sanskrit scholar Pāṇini tells us that we will find the meaning of the root "chit" in: perceiving, noticing, observing, remembering, being aware of, and even shining and caring for.

So, from all of this, what does Sanskrit mean when it refers to "being conscious?"

It means being awake and aware. It means being connected and observant. It means being intelligent, perceptive and understanding. It means attending and taking notice.

It means recognizing what you are doing when you are doing it and acting authentically rather than acting unconsciously, going through the motions pretending you are confident.

We can nod our heads and take all this information for granted. We can assume that we are "awake and aware" because we don't usually walk into lamp posts! However, being conscious encompasses all levels of awareness—awareness of the physical world, the mental world, the emotional world and the spiritual world: it's a 360° awareness.

If we are caught up in one of these worlds, in our mental and emotional stories of events and experiences from the past, then we are not awake and aware of the full picture; we are not really conscious. In a way we are "asleep" while walking around. Remember Shakespeare's genius description at the beginning of this chapter?

> "...This is a strange repose, to be asleep
> With eyes wide open, standing, speaking, moving,
> And yet so fast asleep."

This form of "waking sleep" is a significant limitation. It is not a neutral situation. When we see the world through this screen of waking sleep—standing, speaking, moving, and yet so fast asleep—we can't fully know what's happening, nor are we prepared for what is coming next. This leads naturally to a feeling of uncertainty and anxiety. This anxiety is sticky. It holds in place the limits we have put around ourselves. These limits, unconsciously self-created, cast a shadow over our lives.

We live within a shadow of fear. These limits rule our lives and we unwittingly allow this to happen. Then we wonder why we feel unfulfilled and unhappy. We often project this unhappiness outwards. Without awareness and consciousness of how we impose these limits on ourselves, we blame others and say it's their fault that we feel unhappy.

We like to believe we are aware, but are we? The following story illustrates the limitations of our awareness that we can be blind to.

The Blind Villagers and the Elephant

In a village by the edge of the forest, lived a group of people who were all blind. They all lived in houses next to each other. Every week on the same day, they all gathered together outside and a neighbour would come and tell them the news of the village.

They loved hearing all the comings and goings that had occurred throughout the week. They would spend the rest of the week discussing the events in minute detail.

In one of these weekly news reports, they were told about a new thing that had just arrived in the village called an "elephant." They were all fascinated by it and wanted to learn more.

◆

The following week, the owner of the elephant hearing of the blind villagers, and their interest in the elephant, brought it around to their homes so they could experience it first-hand.

They stood in a circle around the elephant and began to feel the part of the body in front of them. One was standing by the trunk, another by one of the ears, one by a leg, and yet another by the tail. There was a blind villager in front of each part of the elephant.

After the elephant and its owner had departed, they all enthusiastically discussed their experience.

"The elephant is like a big hose," declared the one feeling the trunk.

Another person touching the ear announced, "No, you are mistaken, the elephant is like a fan waving in the breeze."

"How can that be? The elephant in my hands was as a great tree trunk. You must be deluded," pronounced yet another blind villager who had been feeling a leg.

◆

This went on for some time as they all heatedly debated their point of view about their own experience of the elephant. A passer-by, having heard the loud arguments from some distance away, stopped to enquire of the problem.

They reported on the morning's events, and the traveler easily resolved the disagreements.

"The different conclusion that each one of you has reached, is based on a partial experience of the elephant. No-one experienced the whole animal, and therefore none of you has the full picture. The way to know what an elephant is actually like, is to share your knowledge and experience, in order to have a more complete and accurate picture of the truth of an elephant."

The blind villagers laughed at their misunderstanding and enjoyed many happy hours long into the evening sharing all that they had learnt about the elephant.

The message of this story is that our partial and fragmented points of view blind us to reality. They filter our experience through ideas and preferences which have been built up from the past. To have a complete picture of any situation, we need to be awake to the underlying whole that unifies. The unifying factor is our conscious, awake self. Our true self is aware of the whole.

What Is Conscious versus Unconscious Confidence?

Conscious Confidence means that you can freely access confidence, inner strength and self-control whenever you wish. You are able to be confident in a new situation or one that challenges you. You are seeing what is really happening instead of having a partial view like the blind men who were unaware of the other parts of the elephant.

Having Conscious Confidence means being awake to and aware of the truth of any situation. It means being free, connected and in-touch. You have faith in yourself and trust that everything you need to act effectively is available to you in the present moment. You can see potential and opportunities for success. It is a firm foundation for action.

Unconscious Confidence is very different.

Have you ever come across people who appear extremely confident and outspoken, and yet are quite insecure? Perhaps you experience this too. This apparent confidence is unconscious. It is confidence that is experienced by those who are not awake to the truth of a situation and their own experience. It is an outward show of strength. It is brittle and can shatter when events don't go our way.

Unconscious confidence also causes behaviors such as being:

- Brash: Egotistical, "Look at me!", "I'm the center of the universe!", Does all the talking and is unable to listen, "Mansplaining" and "Womansplaining."
- Reckless: Gambling, bravado, stupidity, laddish or frat boy behavior.
- Baseless: Ignorant, convinced that you know something when you don't.
- Impulsive: Acting without proper consideration, taking action before the situation is clear.

These behaviors may appear to indicate confidence at the time, but is it true confidence? Is it confidence rooted in the truth? No, it is unconscious confidence because it doesn't arise from being awake and aware, from intelligent understanding of ourselves and others.

Entering the Heart of Conscious Confidence

The *Bhagavad Gītā* describes the characteristics of a person who has established themselves in "steady wisdom." Steady wisdom is another way of saying Conscious Confidence.

While unconscious confidence comes and goes, Conscious Confidence, based on steady wisdom, doesn't go away.

A person who has steady wisdom, Conscious Confidence, is connected to themselves; they are free, happy and peaceful. They know who they are and what's truly important in life. In every situation they give rather than take, uplift rather than bring down. They know what to do to care for themselves, their family, community, nation and humanity.

This is a person who is unmoved by changing circumstances, by success and failure. They can, therefore, respond and thrive by seeing opportunities where others only see problems.

The starting point for gaining steady wisdom is to establish deep roots within ourselves and to connect with who we really are.

It takes a commitment of body, mind and heart to establish steady wisdom. In fact, it takes the same kind of commitment that anyone who has achieved mastery in any worthwhile field knows about. For example, a ballet dancer, an athlete, or an opera singer understands that it takes knowledge, disciplined training, and effective practice to become expert in their chosen field. Attaining steady wisdom requires the same level of training and commitment.

A Picture of Conscious Confidence

For many years, I studied and worked with a man who was the picture of Conscious Confidence. We spent decades studying and practicing the wisdom traditions, philosophy, Sanskrit and meditation. In addition to being a scholar, he is a husband, father and grandfather.

This man is quietly spoken and never forces himself on situations. Yet, he always brings a clear, strong presence wherever he goes. He is always cheerful. I have never seen him greet anyone, either known or unknown, without a wide smile and a warm-hearted greeting. He makes no distinction about the people he meets. They are all met with the same love, care and attention.

He is highly intelligent, efficient and skilled in many ways both practical and intellectual. He is always full of service; providing anything that is needed no matter how simple. He respects all people, and he is in turn, deeply respected by all who know him. I have seen him respond to many different situations—both public and private—with the same equanimity, lightness of touch, openness and intelligence.

He has consciously devoted his life to applying timeless wisdom every day in all aspects of his life. He demonstrates Conscious Confidence. I have always viewed him as a person of steady wisdom as he shines from a strong connection within himself and his deep abiding spiritual values. He is a true gentleman. He practices being consciously confident.

Practices

Starter Who Am I Now?

Let's start practicing being awake and aware—being conscious.

- Begin by sitting quietly, ideally where you feel calm and still. Focus gently on the breathing without changing anything until your mind settles.

- Now ask yourself: "Who am I now?"
  Let the question go, without looking for an answer.

- Then allow your awareness to settle on your body—become aware of the sensations and energies moving around the body.

- Let your awareness expand to the thoughts and feelings constantly coming and going.

- Now be aware of the feeling that you exist; this underpins all the thoughts and feelings, and the sensations in the body. This is an even quieter awareness.

- Ask the question a few times throughout this exercise: "Who am I now?" This is not about finding an answer.

- In this awareness, note that you can observe the sensations in the body, and the thoughts and feelings in the mind and heart. Rest in this expanded and deeper awareness of yourself for a minute or two.

- Practice this once or twice a day for at least a week. It only takes a few minutes, so there is always enough time.

There are no "ideal" experiences or answers. Be gentle with yourself. This is not an exercise in assessing or criticizing yourself. Any idea of success or failure is just another passing thought and feeling. You are simply being aware, that's all!

The practice of raising awareness is the key point.

Intermediate **Sensory Connection**

Have a journal or some paper and a pen with you.

- Begin by sitting quietly, in a place where you feel calm and still, connect with the breathing for a few moments until your mind settles. Take a moment to relax.

  Now gently let your attention and awareness connect with the senses one at a time.

- Begin by feeling the body sitting in a chair or whatever you are sitting on. Feel the feet, the arms, hands, neck and so on. Feel the body as a whole. Be aware of the warmth and energies moving around the various parts of your body. Become aware of your breathing without changing anything.

- Now connect with sight. Simply let shapes, forms and colours come into view. There's no need to name or label anything.

- Next connect with smell. Let any odours enter the nose without naming them.

- Similarly, with taste.

  If there are no very specific smells or tastes at the time, then rest in the awareness of that neutrality.

- Finally become aware of the hearing. Simply listen. Let sounds enter and let the hearing expand past any thoughts in the mind. Let all of it be appreciated without stopping to engage with it. Let it carry on by itself. Let the hearing expand beyond it.

- If you find yourself caught up in any thoughts and feelings, then gently return to the awareness.

  This simple connection with the senses brings your awareness into the present moment. Practice this awareness in the present moment for a short time, perhaps a minute or two.

There is no success or failure with this exercise. It will be different every time you practice. Do this practice at least twice a day for a minimum of two weeks. Regular practice is the key.

During these two weeks of practice, record your experiences in your journal. Create two headings: the experiences of when you felt centered, still and aware; and when your attention was caught in distractions. Make notes about your experiences. Both observations, being aware and centered or being distracted, are useful. Don't judge yourself negatively if your notes about being distracted are longer than your notes about being aware and attentive.

Advanced Be Aware of Hasty Speech

Take a quiet moment to stop and consider a situation either at work, at home or in a social environment where an unconscious habit of hasty speech takes over.

- Choose just one area—home, work or social.

- Choose just one habit of hasty speech.
  The habit of hasty speech could be for example: interrupting, criticizing or complaining. Consider times where the speech is out of your mouth before you're aware of it. Ideally, choose one verbal habit that happens regularly.

- Now make a firm decision, a resolve, that you will make every effort possible to wait for a few moments before you speak: maybe count to two or three before speaking.

- When the habit comes up, when you are aware of the habit being at the tip of your tongue, that is the time to hold firm to your resolution to wait and watch for a few moments. Let that first habit of speech fall back and see what presents itself to say in that all-important space when you wait.
  It is important to note that you are resolving to wait before speaking. This doesn't mean bottling up speech. The resolve is simply to wait, and let speech arise consciously.

You are bringing greater awareness to an old habit, so that you can apply your reason and intelligence to choose whether to speak it. This is practicing being more conscious, awake and aware. Speech is extremely powerful, so it is a very good place to start. Without such greater awareness, we remain like the blind villagers or the tethered camels perceiving a world of partial reality.

If you forget, don't worry. Just refresh your resolve that you will practice when you do remember.

After a week, it is also highly recommended to sit down and note in your journal what you have noticed about this practice. What has been the effect of being more conscious with one specific habit of speech, in one specific area of your life?

Now let us delve a little deeper into one of the major blockages to Conscious Confidence, that is, the Fear Shadow.

Chapter 4

THE FEAR SHADOW

"Fear is only as deep as the mind allows."

—Japanese proverb

In the previous chapter we addressed the importance of raising our level of consciousness. Now we need to look at some of the challenges that may present themselves. There are several of these, but they are all based on some form of fear.

The Snake and the Rope

Once a young woman was walking down a country lane at dusk. It was neither full sunlight nor the dark of night. There was just enough light for her to stay on the path, no colours were visible, only grey shapes and shadows.

Up ahead she saw something on the road, it was long and thin. A snake!

♦

Her heart pounded, her breathing became shallow and rapid. She was frozen in terror, paralyzed, unable to move forward and fearful of retracing her steps in the gathering dark.

Then she remembered that she had a flashlight in her backpack. With a shaking hand she pulled it out and switched it on. Now she could back away from the danger and try again tomorrow when surely the snake would be gone. First however, she cautiously directed the beam at the fearsome shape lying on the path.

♦

> The moment the light shone on the snake, she saw that it was just an old piece of rope lying on the road, discarded in the dust.
> Relief washed over her. As quickly as the fear had appeared, it evaporated. She chuckled at her foolishness and continued forward on her way, happy and free from fear.
>
> ~ contemporary story, originally told by the philosopher
> Adi Śaṅkara (788 – 820 CE)

We are that young woman, and this story is our story. The road is the journey of our life. The dim light at dusk is the ordinary level of our awareness in which we dwell. The snake represents the entirety of our illusions, our assumptions, jealousies, fears, infatuations, obsessions based on half-understood information and incomplete knowledge. The light from the flashlight is the illumination of true and complete knowledge.

The transformation of our understanding occurs at the instant that wisdom illuminates the situation. The light immediately banishes mistaken understanding, and this dispels the shadow of fear without further effort. This is because the "fear-snake" was never there. It only existed in our imagination. It was only ever a piece of rope dimly lit on the road ahead. The light of knowledge makes that clear and dispels the fear.

What Does Sanskrit Teach Us about Fear?

The Sanskrit word for "fear" is "bhayam."

"Bhayam" (भयम्), meaning fear, alarm, dread, apprehension.

Pāṇini rather curiously tells us that "in fear there is fear."

What can he mean by this? Pāṇini is telling us that you will only experience fear when you are fearful.

In other words, Pāṇini is speaking of fear that feeds upon itself. This fear is essentially irrational. It arises as a sort of nameless dread when some apparent trigger appears, but it collapses when a bit of light is shone on the illusory "cause" of the fear. He is telling us that this kind of fear is its own cause. When we shift our focus, the fear disappears.

This is the kind of fear that President Franklin D. Roosevelt (FDR) spoke of in his inaugural address in 1933, "…let me assert my firm belief that the only thing we have to fear is fear itself – nameless, unreasoning, unjustified terror which paralyses needed efforts to convert retreat into advance."

The fear being referred to is a baseless false emotion that paralyses us or makes us do and say things under its spell. FDR echoed Pāṇini and the ancient Sanskrit wisdom about fear.

It is this kind of fear that Conscious Confidence addresses and banishes. Before we get to how to make that happen, however, let's just look at a couple of different types of fear which are actually useful and do have a basis in reality.

Useful Fear

There are two other types of fear experiences that have their purpose.

The first is the fight-flight response to actual immediate and present danger. This is a survival mechanism.

This fear response is triggered in situations of perceived threat. It floods through the body in an instant. This response is designed to remove us from danger as quickly as possible by flooding our body with adrenaline, clearing our mind of any thinking that is not relevant to the situation. It gets us running away from any immediate threat to life and limb. If danger threatens, this is exactly the response we want!

The second type of useful "fear" experience arises when we are called upon to give a performance or do something in front of others. This form of anticipation prepares us to give our best and can be very useful. It lifts us out of our ordinary considerations, so we can enter the creative "performance space" where the magic can happen. It is a form of respect for our audience. Actors, singers, speakers and dancers know about this space.

However, we all know that it can get out of control and can turn into performance anxiety. Stage fright can paralyze us and interfere with the performance rather than enhance it. The healthy anticipation of a performance is transformed into "snake-fear." Although we are not actually facing the threat of a tiger chasing us across the stage, this is how our bodies and minds react.

This is the type of baseless fear which we now have to address. It is that "snake-fear," that has no basis in reality. I call it the Fear Shadow.

The Fear Shadow

Conscious Confidence is like the sun and the Fear Shadow is like a cloud that conceals the sun; essentially distorting reality. The sun is always there, ever-shining, but on cloudy days it appears as if the sun has vanished. We don't usually think about fear being a shadow. We usually think about fear having its own reality. This assumed reality is simply not true. In fact, the more we grapple with unreal fear, the more it seems to strengthen and grow.

What is this Fear Shadow? What is it made of? What is its effect on us?

Conscious Confidence is founded on being awake and self-aware, but when, through ignorance, we step out of the sunlight into the twilight world of the Fear Shadow, the energy is misused and creates the opposite experience.

So, under the Fear Shadow, instead of connecting with our innermost being and the strength of our core values, we lack self-knowledge and are unclear about who we really are. Instead of a naturally positive attitude, we find ourselves locked in negativity. Under the Fear Shadow courage becomes fear, love becomes cold and aloof, simplicity turns to complication, and creativity becomes narrow and unimaginative.

Many people get caught in this Fear Shadow. In fact, for some people the Fear Shadow can darken their entire life. As in the story of the snake and the rope, if we spend each day in the dimness of our ordinary awareness, we will encounter many imaginary "snakes" on our journey. We will live under the Fear Shadow much of the time.

To survive, we create a "comfort zone" around us. Within that comfort zone, we move, act and speak fairly efficiently. We can run a company or a nation, raise a family or coach a football team.

However, what happens when we are pushed to the edge of that comfort zone? This is when we are tested. At the limits of our comfort zone, we begin to experience unsettling and uncomfortable feelings such as blame, apathy, fear, anger, excuses and a host of others. We all have our default position.

How about the regular meditator who experiences bliss and peace when everything is calm and quiet, but becomes angry and frustrated when their neighbour starts drum practice? Or the high-achieving young woman who is efficient, competent and hard-working, but becomes paralyzed with self-doubt when a colleague passes judgement on her work.

There are talented intelligent people who suffer from social anxiety in new situations. There are brilliant artists who can perform perfectly in the practice studio but find excuses to avoid performing in public.

The list goes on. These are people pushed to the edge of their comfort zone. The edge of our comfort zone is, in fact, an energy barrier that appears at the point where we repeatedly shy away from the unknown, the uncomfortable and the unfamiliar.

This creates the Fear Barrier that maintains an area of apparent efficiency, success, skills and achievement within an invisible limiting sphere, such that when we are pushed by the unfamiliar, the surprising or the challenging, we can go to pieces. This can even lead to our physical and/or mental health being significantly affected. Relationships can suffer, self-esteem can dissolve and so on.

What if we learn to cross the Fear Barrier?

What lies on the other side of the imaginary line?

Freedom, creativity, power, growth and Conscious Confidence.

Through the wisdom of Sanskrit and my own deep practice, I have discovered an effective way to come out from under the Fear Shadow and to cross the Fear Barrier. Instead of calling in the snake charmers, I propose a visit to the flashlight store!

The process is to turn our attention away from the fear, and instead establish ourselves in the light of wisdom. This is the light which transforms all our illusory snakes into harmless pieces of rope. It allows us to walk confidently and courageously forward on our path to happiness, strength, success and fulfillment.

Crossing the Fear Barrier

Picture a woman. From the outside she looks ordinary enough, medium height, attractive, accomplished. She is heading off to work at her job in a school where she has been teaching children for many years.

However, she has a secret.

When she was the age of the children she now teaches, about nine years old, she was introduced to spiritual wisdom. Her parents, also seekers after eternal truths and a life lived with purpose, created a home life for this young lady and her siblings, which from one angle looked ordinary, suburban, and conventional. However, from the point of view of the inner life of the seeker after wisdom, it was a home full of excitement, adventure, discussion and discovery.

Unusually for one so young she fell in love with the spiritual knowledge and the training which came her way. She was guided by family and friends and fellow seekers and she was eager to learn.

She discovered such marvels as the philosophical underpinnings of ordinary life. Also, she was taught meditation, stillness, and other practical techniques and disciplines essential for living a life with purpose and meaning. She performed simple exercises that cultivated the heart, the mind and the spirit. These exercises included the application of focused attention, the ability to persevere, to care for others, and to go deep within her own being.

This created a rich inner life, all while she attended high school, university and ultimately took up a place as a teacher of children.

For many years she happily undertook her responsibilities as an educator, and also continued to spend much time under spiritual guidance and discipline. While some effort and sometimes uncomfortable self-examination were necessary parts of her journey, she felt safe and secure in the company of her fellow seekers after spiritual wisdom.

Even from a very young age, she had an enduring sense that everything she was taught, and everything presented for her to do was preparing her for something; but it was never clear to her what this "something" was.

After many years, she began to feel a niggling sense of constriction. It was a bit confusing at first. She applied the techniques, the meditation and awareness to this feeling. However, it persisted.

Then one day she was meditating, and she made a life-changing decision. She stopped meditating and gave the feeling of unease her full attention. Instead of resisting it and trying to move it on from her heart and mind, she welcomed it and began to ask herself: What are you trying to tell me? What do I have to learn from you?

She found it was telling her that it was time to discover her unique self. In order to do that, she knew she had to relinquish all the safeties and certainties of the structures and even the company of the people she had been with for decades. If she was ever to discover and fulfil the "something" she was destined for, she had to go free and step into the unknown.

She had to turn from all the structures and relationships which had been so helpful and fruitful in her journey. She was being guided by an inner voice to turn inwards and discover for herself an inner voice of authority.

This was exciting but at the same time unknown and frightening. She hadn't known anything other than a very structured environment her whole life. She realized that it was time to follow this new energy arising from within herself; follow it wherever it led.

Her thoughts were telling her things like:

"This is just ego, stay with what has worked in the past. The future is unsure and unclear." "You're stepping away from a protected environment, it's not safe."

"You won't be able to do this."

"What if you are wrong? What if it fails? What if you fail?"

All this might have sapped her enthusiasm or had her retreating into her familiar comfort zone. The biggest barrier to overcome at this point was fear. Despite these murmurings of fear, she couldn't deny the power and clarity of the new energy that was arising within her. It didn't push, and it wasn't forceful. It was still, strong, clear, and benevolent; it had an undeniable presence and made her feel limitless, happy and powerful.

Through her regular meditation practice, the distinction between these two energies—the old and the new—became clearer and clearer.

She felt happy, alive, positive and enthusiastic when she followed the new voice telling her to step into her own unique self. The old space of her comfort zone, staying under the external guidance of others, left her feeling like she was living in a grey formulaic past. She was, however, grateful for the structure and direction which had taken her to the threshold of this new phase in her journey.

The crucial revolutionary step was an inner decision to simply trust and follow faithfully that enlivening energy no matter where it led, how long it took or what was presented on the way.

She said a happy and warm farewell to the organization which had given her so much on her journey. She retired from teaching, to the equally warm praises of her colleagues, students and their families. She took up many other pursuits. Some of them were things she had wanted to do for many years, others were a surprise.

Her one wish was to create something so that others could benefit from all she had been taught, all she had learned, all she had mastered. This required her saying "Yes" to each opportunity as it arose.

With each "Yes," her comfort zone, which had already been tested quite a bit, was put under further challenge. This wasn't always easy, but her years of meditation practice, perseverance, knowledge and discipline came to the rescue every time. At each point, when she broke through that comfort zone and went beyond the Fear Barrier, new opportunities, new energy and new potential were unlocked.

One day out of the blue, she was contacted by a woman offering her the opportunity to host her own radio show. She didn't see that coming!

Since then she has been developing this opportunity to get the message of Conscious Confidence out to the world. She has even been asked to write a book. That book is the one you are now holding in your hands. When we develop Conscious Confidence, our fears fall away and lose their power, and we have greater clarity to see and take up opportunities that we would otherwise not even contemplate.

Practices

All the practices in this chapter are a way of turning on the flashlight before the dimness of twilight turns to night. If we strengthen ourselves through knowledge, wisdom and practice, then we will have the resilience and resources when we need them to step clear of the Fear Barrier and stay in the light of our true magnificent self.

The best time to practice is when you don't seem to need it. Establish a practice in the easy times so you're strong and prepared for the challenging times. Easy times are for practice, so that we are ready in the challenging times. This is how we learn and grow. We have to be like the runner, or the public speaker who prepares before the main event.

So, what should we practice? In this chapter the practices are designed to establish ready access to stillness. Stillness is the key quality to nurture within yourself.

Where fear is concerned, it may seem counter-intuitive to practice inner stillness. However, fear is dependent on movement; it is a form of constant activity. Therefore, the antidote is stillness. The power and light of knowledge which turns the "fear-snake" into a rope, comes from this strong inner still point.

Your practice of stillness will weaken the fear and make you steady and resilient. Having access to inner stillness, will allow you to grow and discover new potential within yourself.

Starter The Anchor

The Anchor can help you establish a strong and steady inner still point. This still point is a place inside yourself beyond the chatter and unsteadiness of the mind, and the constantly changing feelings. It is still, calm, silent, and peaceful. It is a point from which you can observe the world accurately and from which you can readily respond to take effective action.

Practice this exercise at least once or twice a day for two minutes. Try to make this a regular part of your life. Start with two weeks.

- Sit comfortably and relaxed in a chair.

- Keep your eyes open; let yourself perceive forms, shapes and colours without naming them.

- Slowly take a deep breath in, and then exhale.
  Repeat this slow deep breathing twice more, relaxing each time you exhale.

- Become aware of your body sitting in the chair.
  - Feel your feet touching the floor.
  - Feel your clothes touching your skin.
  - Feel the air touching your face and hands.

- Let the listening open wide and expand; listen past any thoughts in the mind; listen without naming any of the sounds.

- Expand your awareness to include all sounds, people, objects, the entire environment and beyond.

Intermediate 1 The Observer

This exercise is for developing equanimity in the face of changing emotions.
Practice this exercise at least once a day for two minutes:

- Sit comfortably and relaxed in a chair.

- Slowly take a slow deep breath in, and then exhale.
  Repeat this slow deep breathing twice more, relaxing each time you exhale.

- Come to an inner still point and rest there.

- Stay present to feelings, all feelings; watch them rise and fall.
  Stay present without any commentary or narrative about the feelings.

- Remain still and present to the feelings; if commentaries, opinions and judgments arise, let them pass too.

- Stay present and watching as a witness, or observer, to all the feelings.

Watching and witnessing without preference is the key; the feelings may be positive and blissful, negative and uncomfortable, or relatively neutral; keep allowing them to rise and fall whilst remaining still as the witness.

Intermediate 2 **The Flashlight**

This exercise is adapted from the ***Taittiriya Upanishad***. It involves switching on the flashlight of wisdom.
Practice this exercise at least twice a day.

- Stop what you are doing for a moment. Take at least one deep relaxing breath.

- Think of someone you know or someone you have heard of who you consider to be wise.

- Ask yourself deliberately: "What would that wise man or woman think now?" The questioning is the important thing; release any expectation of any particular answer and stay open and still.

Advanced **Expansion**

The previous exercises, The Anchor, The Observer and the Flashlight, are designed to be practiced in both the easy times, and when challenges strike.

This practice, Expansion, is for the times when you are pushed to the edge of your comfort zone. Together with the other three practices, it is here to help you build up your muscle to cross the Fear Barrier.

The Expansion exercise is about remaining present and still, while listening beyond those emotions which appear at the outer limits of the Fear Barrier. These emotions can drive us back into our comfort zone.

Practice this when you feel the challenge of being pushed to the edge of your comfort zone.

- Stop what you are doing and become grounded by feeling your feet on the floor. Become aware of your whole body from top to toe even while feeling under pressure. This brings you into the present moment.

- Take a slow deep breath in, and then slowly exhale. Repeat this slow deep breathing twice more, relaxing each time you exhale.

- Come to an inner stillness. Witness the challenging emotional responses in the body and mind. This may take a little time to settle into, so keep breathing, remaining aware and watching as the emotions play out.

- Then let the listening expand past the thoughts and feelings in the body and mind, feel yourself expanding and growing larger than the emotional reactions. Feel that the awareness encompasses those emotional challenges.

- Every time the attention and listening are drawn back into the emotions, gently release again and open up the awareness and listening as you keep letting go.

You may find it useful to try this exercise while engaged in gentle walking. The physical activity can help to redirect the energy from the challenging feelings.

Introduction to the F.U.S.E. Program

The F.U.S.E. Program is a practical step by step guide to take us on a journey out from under the Fear Shadow to a world of Conscious Confidence. It has six elements: Core Values, Positive Attitude, and the Four-Fold Energy of Conscious Confidence comprising Focusing, Uniting, Simplifying, and Energizing. Each of these six elements is dealt with in a subsequent chapter, beginning with Core Values. Each of these six elements has a Key Practice which the Starter, Intermediate and Advanced practices fill out.

Chapter Five

CORE VALUES

"In this body, in this town of Spirit, there is a little house shaped like a lotus, and in that house there is a little space. One should know what is there. What is there? Why is it so important? There is as much in that little space within the heart, as there is in the whole world outside. Heaven, earth, fire, wind, sun, moon, lightning, stars; whatever is and whatever is not, everything is there."

—Shrī Purohit Swāmi and W. B. Yeats,
Chandogya Upanishad, The Ten Principal Upanishads

Once we are able to leave the Fear Shadow behind us, it is easier to begin considering what lies in that space in the heart beyond all fear. That space within the heart contains all our possibilities. In that space we can discover what is of the highest importance to us, what we truly value. In English the word "value"—worth, price, importance—carries many levels of meaning. At the most superficial level we all have certain things we value above other things, in the clothes we choose, the places we visit, even the movies we watch. We are making judgments and choices at this level all day, often without realizing it.

At a deeper level, we have our "Core Values" such as freedom or tolerance or fair-play. These deeper values govern the studies we pursue, the profession we choose to join, our political ideology, the friends we associate with, the partner we choose for life, and the way we educate our children.

The living out of these Core Values may appear to change and evolve as we take our journey through life; however, it is actually our understanding, experience and expression of our Core Values that develops and grows. For example, if one of our Core Values were Honesty, the expression of that essential ideal would be different when we were six years old, when we were a teenager and when we reached maturity.

To take an analogy, our Core Values are like the sun, and how we live out those values is like the rays of the sun.

The following story illustrates the importance of Time in coming to an understanding of values, in this case Love.

An Island Vacation

Long ago all the Attributes, Values and Qualities gathered together for a restful holiday on a beautiful tropical island. They were all invited, none were excluded. Everyone was enjoying themselves in the glorious weather. Wisdom, Understanding and Temperance sat under palm trees and talked for hours. Courage, Resolution and Resilience went on long and challenging treks around the island. Stillness, Tranquility and Peace soaked up the sun and spent each day resting and meditating. Impatience, Judgment and Anger stormed off arguing as usual. Everyone was having a wonderful time!

◆

After a few days, news came of a huge tropical storm heading for the island. They all had to leave immediately.

The peaceful scene turned to panic as they gathered their belongings and rushed to find boats to take them to safety on the mainland. There was one boat for each Attribute, so everyone climbed into one of the waiting fleet of vessels. All that is, except Love, who was the last to realize that it was time to leave.

However, there was a problem. Someone had miscounted. There weren't any boats left. Love looked around to see what could be done. The first to sail by was Prosperity. Love called out, "Can you please give me a lift back to the mainland?" Prosperity replied, "So sorry but my boat is completely full of all my precious possessions and wealth which I must get back to safety without fail."

Prosperity sailed away.

◆

Then Vanity sailed by in a very stylish boat, so Love tried again, "Please can you give me a ride back to safety?" Vanity replied, "No, your feet are muddy and dirty, and you're wet. You will mess up my expensive and top-class boat."

So, Vanity also sailed away leaving Love alone.

♦

Love waited a little while for another boat to pass and behold, along came Sorrow. Love called out, "Oh please dear Sorrow, can you help me? Please take me back to the mainland." Sorrow looked up and said, "No sorry, this is all too awful. I don't want any company at the moment, I want to be by myself."

So, Sorrow sailed away leaving Love on the island.

♦

Happiness was in the next boat to come by. Love called out, "Hello Happiness, can you please let me travel with you back to shore and away from this storm?" Happiness was having such a good time in the excitement of rushing around packing and getting off the island! Love's request for help went unnoticed. It was just all too much fun!

By now the storm was getting closer and the sky was darkening with threatening clouds. Lightning flashed and strong winds whipped up the water and sand.

♦

Suddenly Love heard a voice call out, "Quickly, get in my boat! I will take you back to the mainland and out of this storm." Love jumped into the boat, but in the darkness and confusion couldn't see who had offered help. When safely off the island, Love sought out Wisdom and asked, "Who saved me when everyone else turned away? Who rescued me from the island?"

♦

Wisdom smiled, "That was Time. Only Time knows the true value of Love. Only Time knows what Love can do. Time knows that only Love can bring real peace, happiness and prosperity."

The message of this story is we miss out on love if we become too fixated on prosperity, or happiness, or sorrow, or anything really! Only with time, do we come to understand the true value and power of love.

We should examine our values and be clear about them, so that there is a balance and we can experience a full range of positive values and qualities.

The following ancient tale is from the *Mahābharata* by Vālmīki. The *Mahābharata* is the longest epic poem ever written. Dating from around the 8th or 9th centuries BCE, it consists of over 100,000 verses in Sanskrit.

This story of five princely brothers is an allegory of the fundamental values and virtues that we all carry in our hearts.

The Five Sons of King Pandu

Long ago in ancient India lived a wise and brave King named Pandu. He had two intelligent and beautiful wives, Queen Kuntī and Queen Madrī. They lived happily as Pandu ruled his kingdom wisely and led his armies to victory.

All seemed happy and peaceful until one day Pandu was cursed. He would be unable to father any children with his Queens. King Pandu was grief stricken because he could no longer ensure the continuation of the royal line. So, he abdicated the throne in favour of his brother.

King Pandu, Queen Kuntī and Queen Madrī retired to the forest to live holy lives in prayer and acts of charity.

◆

Then everything changed for King Pandu, because Queen Kuntī had a secret. Many years before, she had been granted a secret gift. If she ever called up any of the gods, then that god would appear before her and she could bear his son. Kunti had been very careful not to call on any of the gods!

◆

Now, however, she told her secret to King Pandu and Queen Madrī. Pandu was overjoyed and begged Kuntī to call upon the great god Yama, lord of justice, law and death. Her first son, born of Yama, was called Prince Yudhishthira. He was known for his qualities of honesty, justice and discernment.

She then called on the Lord Vāyu, the mighty god of the wind. Her second son was Prince Bhīma. He was huge and powerful and had an enormous appetite! He was the strongest champion of goodness and truth.

Finally, Kuntī called on Lord Indra himself, the king of the gods. Her third son was Prince Arjuna. He excelled at leadership and was an inspiration to his followers.

◆

Madrī begged Kuntī to share her secret so she too could be the mother of princes. So Kuntī whispered the secret prayer into Madrī's ear.

Madrī summoned the Ashwins, the twin gods who bestowed the treasures of health and wealth. The Ashwins shone with beauty and light like the sunrise and sunset.

Madrī gave birth to twin sons, the radiant Princes Nakula and Sahadeva. Nakula had the special power of diplomacy, and Sahadeva could see into the future.

◆

Thus, Kuntī gave birth to three of the five princes—Yudhishthira, Bhīma and Arjuna—and Madrī gave birth to the other two, Nakula and Sahadeva.

◆

These five princes, fathered by the gods themselves, were known as the five sons of King Pandu. These princes, who embodied the powers of righteousness, strength, lordliness, compassion and wisdom, were destined to defeat evil and restore peace, prosperity and harmony in their kingdom.

◆

This story illustrates a central point about Core Values. Your values are innate, they form an essential element of who you are. If you are kind and considerate, you value these qualities at your core, and they colour you and your world. If you value honor and dignity, you will be a different person from someone who values compassion, and another who values knowledge, and another who values efficiency and success.

The power of our essential values is indicated in the story by the divine godly powers which were imparted into each son. They were not human powers, they came from the divine world.

Whatever your values, they will pervade and colour your whole life experience like a drop of ink in a glass of water. The ink doesn't stay in one corner of the glass, the entire glass of water is coloured by the ink.

What Does Sanskrit Teach Us about Values?

Sanskrit has several words that mean "value." Two of these, which carry profound and practical meaning, are "mūlyam" and "argha." The first word "mūlyam," means your system of self-belief, the values that are the root or foundation of who you are. The second word, "argha," means the qualities or virtues that you honor and respect above all others. Let's explore the deeper meanings of these two Sanskrit words.

Mūlyam (मूल्यम्), the fundamental value, being at the root, the origin. To plant and grow strong.

This first word for value—Mūlyam—has a meaning related to origins, strong roots, planting and growing firm. There is nothing weak, feeble or vulnerable about mūlyam.

What are these firm roots? They are our Core Values, the values at the core of our being, our system of self-belief. How we live our lives and the choices we make are determined by what we value. Therefore, it is essential to be clear about what our Core Values are.

Pāṇini tells us that we can discover our fundamental values, our firm roots, by examining those areas in our life where we are creative, where we flourish, succeed and are prosperous, on all levels. A plant that is healthy and flourishing, must have firm, strong and healthy roots. For example, if you are drawn to the creative world of drama and succeed and flourish as a playwright, or if you have prospered and flourished in commerce, or as a teacher, then by finding out what drew you to that area of creative activity, what desire was at the heart of your success, then that will be a good clue to the root and origin of your Core Values.

In fact, one way of discovering our Core Values is to work backwards in this way by looking at those areas in our life which are creative and successful. What is it that gets our attention and our energy? What flourishes in our life because we commit to them? Is it our family, our work, our friendships, our study, our spiritual journey?

Argha (अर्घ) value, worth, price. To honor, to worship. The respectful reception of a guest.

This second word for "value" has an emotional dimension as well as an association with specific actions. Pāṇini indicates that we can discover what we really value by asking what it is that we honor, respect and worship, where we hold nothing back. We could, for example, honor and respect Love, Generosity, Strength or Service.

Here we are considering what we honor, venerate and worship in our heart. The heart has a powerful capacity to honor, respect and worship. In fact, we are always honoring, respecting and worshipping something. The question then is, what is the object of our honor and respect? This is where the analogy of the guest comes in. What is it that we welcome into our heart? What values receive a warm embrace?

The school where I used to teach had five Core Values: Stillness, Truth, Courage, Service and Respect. To inculcate these values, we encouraged the students to ask themselves: Am I awake and aware? Do I respond to others who need my help? Can I forgive others? The idea was to motivate positive action, and the ultimate aim was to develop a feeling of honor and respect for the values themselves. This is Argha.

This chapter on Core Values opened with a quote from the *Chandogya Upanishad*: This describes the ancient wisdom tradition's view of the heart. It contains everything, the whole universe, all possibilities, everything that we hold dear and value, everything we welcome as a guest into our hearts.

What we hold dear—our Core Values—are very powerful. Whatever we value grows and flourishes. If generosity is something we value, then we will grow in generosity and discover more and more about this positive life-affirming value. Similarly, with honesty, or kindness, or courage. The more we value them, the more our thoughts, feelings and actions reflect that particular Core Value.

It is also true that not everything we value is necessarily positive. If, for example, greed, selfishness and spite are given our emotional energy, they too will grow and our thoughts, feelings and actions will reflect these narrow and negative values.

It is therefore so important to be aware of what we value. It is clearly better for us and those around us that we honor and revere positive and favorable attributes. The guests that we welcome with respect into the home in our heart should be life-affirming and positive.

Volunteering is a wonderful example of values in action. When we volunteer, we apply to everyday life the energetic quality of the two Sanskrit words for value: Mūlyam, establishing a firm foundation of value; and Argha, honoring others and treating others with respect. Volunteering demonstrates working with and for others without any thought of getting something in return, honoring them and treating them as revered guests.

There are so many inspiring examples of volunteer work, however I have chosen two from Australia that have inspired me. I'm sure you can also think of many more wonderful examples. You may be a volunteer in your community, and if so, I salute you for that.

Orange Sky Australia

In late 2014 two twenty-year old friends, Nic Marchesi and Lucas Patchett of Brisbane, Queensland, decided to improve hygiene standards and restore some dignity to the homeless. They called their enterprise Orange Sky Australia.

They installed two second-hand washing machines and dryers in the back of their old van and drove around parks in Brisbane to offer a free laundry service. The machines kept breaking, and they had to ask their mothers how much laundry powder to put in.

Eventually they got everything working. Their friends thought they were crazy, and that no one would want to wash their clothes in a park, but Nic and Lucas were confident that the idea would work. They began putting out folding chairs for people to sit on while their clothes were being washed and dried. Naturally they engaged the homeless people in conversation whilst they waited. The young men noticed that people felt better about themselves when they were wearing clean clothes; however, the real magic was in the time and care given to listening and conversation. This made the real difference.

Orange Sky Australia has grown into something so much bigger and more powerful than the two young men had ever conceived back in their garage. It has expanded around the country with many more vans, and even offers a shower service. It is staffed by volunteers who treat other people as they would like to be treated themselves and put aside time to connect with people in an open and non-judgmental conversation.

Nic Marchesi and Lucas Patchett were jointly awarded the "Young Australian of the Year" in 2016.

New South Wales Rural Fire Service (NSWRFS)

Australia has large areas of native bushland. In summer during the bush-fire season, this presents a major hazard and significant risk to life and property. The NSWRFS, founded in 1896, is a vast organization dedicated to putting out fires in rural areas.

This essential service is staffed predominantly by volunteers, called "firies" or "bushies." They are highly trained and put themselves at considerable risk to serve communities during the summer season. During the winter they train hard and engage in hazard reduction controlled burning to reduce the risk in summer. If a "fiery" is on duty or on stand-by, they drop everything and go where they are needed, including remote areas nowhere near their local community.

I have had first-hand experience of the NSWRFS when there was a bush fire close to the school where I taught. It was a very hot Friday after-noon and there was the characteristic smell, hanging low in the air, of smoke from a bushfire. The sky was dark and threatening. The children and I could see out the window that there was a fire fairly close by. The school principal phoned the NSWRFS. They were already aware of the fire and were calling in various brigades and the police to attend. Soon NSWRFS fire trucks arrived and set up their operations. The commander liaised with our school principal about safely evacuating the children. At all times they were professional, organized, calm and reassuring. In the space of a few hours, using water-carrying helicopters, they had the fire under control and all lives and properties were safe. We offered to make tea and coffee for them, but their crew included a catering station where volunteers made tea, coffee and sandwiches for everyone. That's all part of the service.

It was a very impressive operation from start to finish and predominantly staffed by volunteers. The NSWRFS even has a Welfare Fund which is funded through donations and fund-raising activities such as a Ball. The Welfare fund operates discreetly to help NSWRFS families who may have fallen on hard times. Another great example of practical and anonymous service from the heart.

The previous two stories show how people take their Core Values and give them practical expression through volunteering. The following practices are designed to allow you to discover your own Core Values, and the Advanced Practice deals with the practical expression of them. Have your journal with you because the exercises include noting down your research, your thoughts and reflections, so that you can later consider them further. The Key Practice in this chapter and subsequent ones is the over-arching aim of the following specific exercises.

Practices

Key Being Self-Aware and Self-Connected

Starter Exploring Values

In this starter practice, we're going to use a volunteer organization to trigger our self-reflection on our own Core Values.

- Think of one volunteer organization that you've heard about and appeals to you. Consider the values of that organization. Orange Sky for example is based on respect and dignity, and the NSWRFS values protection of life and property. Other organizations may value service, care or compassion. If the organization that you select doesn't have any stated values, then reflect on what you feel to be the values that underpin their mission, and what they do.

- Write down three to five values of this organization. For example, in the case of Orange Sky the list might expand to include: respect, dignity, compassion, care and service.

- Research the meanings of each of the listed values of your selected organization. Find out more about the meanings of each of those words, so you broaden and deepen your understanding of those values. There is always more to learn. This exercise helps us to transcend any assumptions. For example, look up a dictionary, a thesaurus or Google to find out a broader range of meanings and usage. You might look up each word on quotation websites to find out how, for example, Shakespeare, Oprah Winfrey or Martin Luther King used the word. Make some notes in your journal of your research.

- Now once you've done this research into the meanings of these 3 to 5 values, take some time to consider your notes and think about these values. Ask yourself the following questions:
    - What is it about these values that draws me to them?
    - What is it about these values that makes them significant to me?
    - What other examples can I recall of these values in action? You might remember something you did, or some action of a family member, a co-worker, a neighbour or someone in your community.

The most important part of this exercise is to expand your understanding. This is achieved by delving deeper into the meaning of the values and asking questions. Answers may or may not come. The questions are what count.

Intermediate Discovering Your Own Core Values

We have been looking at values throughout this chapter. This has included introducing the concept of Core Values: the values we honor and treasure and hold dear, and which form the root and basis of how we live, think, act and speak.

For many of us, however, it is not easy to articulate what our own Core Values are. The aim of this exercise is for you to begin the process of uncovering and giving a name to your own Core Values.

- First, think of the many values we have looked at in this chapter, including those in the list you made in the Starter Practice. Think of as many other values as you can and write them all down. The list can be as long as you like. Here's some to get you started:
"Understanding.....Courage.....Generosity.....Integrity.....Kindness.....Love..."

- Now run your eye down your list and circle those values that you feel a connection with, that "speak" to you, or that are reflected in your actions. Where do you flourish? Where are you creative? Where would you like to find success?

- Now write down in a separate list those values that you have circled. If you have only circled one or two, then that's fine. However, if you have circled ten or twenty, it's probably better to reduce the list to no more than five of your favorites.

[Advanced] Taking Your Core Values into Action

Take out your list of Core Values from the previous practice.

- Now ask yourself:
  - How do I give expression to these values in my life?
  - How can I do more to live out these values?
  - Is there anyone I know, or know of, who is a good example of living out these values?

- Make notes in your journal including some form of "action plan" for taking your Core Values into action in your life. For example, you might reach out to a local service organization and volunteer your time, you might help out a friend or colleague who is in need of a kind word or some practical assistance, or you might resolve to have that honest courageous conversation you have been avoiding.

Our consideration of our Core Values has essentially been inward looking. We look into our own being, into our heart, to discover what we truly value. The Advanced Practice began the move to take these Core Values outwards to the world in which we live and operate. In the next chapter we will look at the lens through which we see the world. This lens can be summarized as our attitude: our point of view, intent and conduct. Our attitude can be positive or negative. The next chapter looks at the powerful effect of a positive attitude to create a world of creativity, certainty, clarity and success.

Chapter Six

POSITIVE ATTITUDE

"Attitude is a little thing that makes a big difference."
—Winston Churchill

This chapter deals with attitude, particularly developing and fostering a positive attitude. In the last chapter we spoke about Core Values and began a process of discovering and putting our own Core Values into action. Now, with the consideration of a Positive Attitude we can accelerate and intensify the practical expression of our Core Values.

Core Values form the basis of who we are, and Positive Attitude is the lens through which those values flow to manifest themselves in the world. You can have the most profound values in your heart, but your attitude to yourself, to others, and to life are the key to making them visible, practical and useful.

Attitude as we shall see, has three aspects. The first is our viewpoint. This is the standpoint from which we view the world. Attitude forms our stance, our perspective, the point of observation. The second aspect of attitude is our intent. What is our motivation for our thoughts and actions? What is it that we are seeking to achieve in our approach to life? The third aspect is conduct. What do we actually do to carry our values and attitude into action? This conduct flows from our viewpoint and our intent.

A Positive Attitude leaves us energized and motivated to deal profitably with the world, generously with ourselves, and with compassion and even forgiveness for events and people that come our way. We see opportunities where others see blockages, and bridges where others see barriers. A Positive Attitude is thus an essential key to success.

The first story illustrates how small a shift it takes to turn our attitude from a negative heavy burden to a light and positive way forward.

What Do You See?

It was a regular day in class. The students drifted in and took their seats. The low hum of chat and shuffling of papers filled in the spare moments until the professor arrived. He was a well-regarded teacher at this University; he'd been teaching there for twenty-five years. So, on this mid-semester day, no one was anticipating anything out of the ordinary.

The professor came in and set his papers down on the front desk as always. His fingers reached into his inside coat pocket to retrieve his glasses. Once they were resting at the end of his nose, he was ready to begin as usual.

"Good Morning class. Please prepare for a test."

♦

A test! No one had said anything about a test today! This was meant to be a regular class. Anxiety swept through the room, changing the atmosphere instantly.

The professor placed a test paper face down on each desk. Once back at the front of the room, he asked everyone to turn their paper over and begin the test.

♦

The students turned their papers over and stared in astonishment. All they could see was a black dot in the middle of a white page. There were no questions or diagrams, no instructions—nothing at all!

The professor looked around the room at the face of each student, noting their puzzled looks. "What do you see? I want you to write what you see."

After ten minutes, he asked everyone to stop writing. There were audible sounds of relief at this instruction. He collected the papers and proceeded to read the answers out aloud.

Everyone had described, in forensic detail, the black dot on the page.

♦

When the professor had finished reading out the last paper, there was total silence in the room. No one knew what to make of this.

"Don't worry, I'm not going to grade these test papers. I just wanted to give you a chance at seeing another perspective. All of you only wrote about the black dot. What about the white paper surrounding it? Most of the paper is white with only a very small part covered by the black dot. Now think about your life. Most of your life is like the white paper, but we spend most of our time focused on a small black dot.

"There are black dots in life, I'm not denying that. However, most of the time life is full of blessings, wonders and gifts. What about your family and friends? You have the gift of education, food, health and safety.

"Why not choose to appreciate and celebrate these wonderful riches in your life each day? Why spend your life focused on tiny black dots such as the money you don't have for something you don't really need, or the issue you're having with a member of your family, or some disagreement you've had with a friend?

"The dark spots are not that numerous, and they are so small in relation to the vast opportunities, gifts and miracles in your life. Why do you allow them to dominate your lives?

"Choose a different perspective. You can do this right now; it takes no time at all. Enjoy your life and all the blessings that it so generously provides each and every day."

Attitude is powerful. A change of attitude can literally change your world and your life. This is because our attitude is like the lens through which we see the world and process its influences. In a challenging situation, one person, with a positive attitude, might see solutions and opportunities for learning and growth, while another, in the exact same situation might have the wind taken out of their sails and retreat into pessimistic inaction. The next story illustrates this well.

The Frog Race

Once there was a large colony of very small frogs. They were looking for a challenge, so they decided to hold a race. There was a tall tower nearby, so everyone agreed that the race would be to the top.

Everything was arranged, and the day of the race arrived. A large crowd of spectators gathered to watch. Most of the spectators didn't really believe that these tiny frogs would actually reach the top of this very tall tower. They were calling out saying:

"The tower is too tall! You're too small. You'll collapse with exhaustion before the top!"

"There's no chance you can reach the top and win."

♦

Well, many of the frogs did collapse from exhaustion. There were some who were stronger than others, so they kept climbing. They could hear the crowd below calling out: "It's too hard, stop before you collapse!" One by one, even the stronger frogs had to give up. The spectators' discouraging shouts were growing louder and louder as more frogs were so tired they had to stop.

♦

There was one tiny frog who kept climbing higher and higher. He didn't stop; he kept going at a steady pace and eventually reached the top. He was the winner! How did he succeed when other much stronger frogs collapsed?

♦

Everyone gathered around the tiny frog and all spoke at once. What was the secret of his success? How did he find the strength to keep going?

The tiny frog held up his hand and called for silence. Then he reached into his ears and pulled out a pair of earplugs. Everyone was astonished. Why was he wearing earplugs?

♦

The frog explained: "I heard people talking before the race, saying that they didn't believe any frog could climb the tower. I had already decided that I was going to reach the top, and I didn't want to have my resolve weakened by the crowd shouting out their negative and limiting opinions. In this way I was able to achieve my goal. I wasn't affected by the pessimistic words because I couldn't hear them!"

What Does Sanskrit Teach Us about Positive Attitude?

There are three Sanskrit words for attitude, all of which can help us understand how to remain positive. The first Sanskrit word is "sthiti," that speaks of our point of view. The second word is "bhāva," that deals with the intent or motivation with which we act. The third Sanskrit word is "vritti," that deals with right conduct. Let's discover each of these three Sanskrit words and their deeper meanings.

Sthiti (स्थिति) Our attitude is our point of view, the stance from which we view the world; our belief system, our convictions.

Bhāva (भाव) Attitude as in our emotional response to whatever we meet; also our intent and motivation for our actions.

Vritti (वृत्ति) Conduct. Attitude as reflected in our behavior; especially in right conduct.

Point of View or Sthiti

The Sanskrit root for our "stance or point of view" is "sthā." This root is all about "standing, staying, stationing oneself and remaining." It is like our "home," the place from which we go out into the world, and to which we return.

Pāṇini tells us that we experience "standing" by "going" and "returning." This seems odd, as "going" and "returning" appear to contradict "standing" and "staying," but the key concept here is going from, and returning to "home." Home is where we live and take our rest and nourishment. It is where we keep our precious possessions. It is our base of operations. We leave home to go to work, to go to school and to interact with others. It is the place we return to when the day is done. It is always the same place. Going out and returning indicate the sort of staying and stationing of ourselves that we do regarding our home, where we live. This is the deeper meaning of "Sthiti," our stance or point of view.

So, the first thing we have to do to understand how to cultivate a positive attitude is to see our stance or point of view as our "home," so to speak. We return to this stance or point of view each time. Our attitude is stationed here. We feel "at home" with this point of view.

Intent or Bhāva

The Sanskrit root of bhāva is "bhū." This means "to be" and "to become." "Bhū" has a wide range of meanings but Pāṇini helps us to narrow them down. He tells us that we will discover the meaning of the root "bhū" in pure existence, in goodness and in excellence. In other words, "bhū" refers to our highest and best self.

To develop the kind of attitude spoken of as bhāva—our motivation for right action and our positive response to events—we must connect with the best and most refined feelings, thoughts and actions that we are capable of. For example, if we have a problem at work, such as discovering that a person in a junior position earns more than we do, then the most reasonable, compassionate and equitable response of which we are capable, will be an exercise in bhāva.

Conduct or Vritti

Another Sanskrit word for "attitude" is "vritti" which means "conduct." Attitude is not merely good intentions or a positive point of view. Attitude must, according to the timeless wisdom of Sanskrit, result in action. The action required is good conduct based on our values, our good intent and a positive point of view.

So, to summarize, if we are to adopt a positive attitude, we must stand in a self-aware point of view, have an intent for the good, and conduct ourselves in ways that reflect both.

Once you gain a taste for a positive attitude and the benefits it brings, once that is your "home," you wouldn't live anywhere else.

"We Appear to Have Another Opportunity"

The Principal and Deputy-Principal, at the school where I taught, were two remarkable men. They were both highly intelligent and demonstrated the real meaning of being life-long learners. They "walked the talk" professionally and personally.

Both studied and researched constantly about new and best practices in relation to education. They were forever looking for new content and how best to deliver this to the students. They were always keen to increase their skills and that of the teaching staff. This made it a very stimulating and exciting place to work. We, the teachers, were always learning too.

In addition, these two men were constantly studying and pursuing their own interests such as math, science, history, Latin, humanities, art and sculpture; the list seemed to be endless. They were also interested in outdoor and physical pursuits such as hiking, rock climbing or dancing. They would always relate some fascinating book or article they had read or something they had done in their spare time. These two leaders were open and looking for new and creative approaches to things. If any staff member, either teaching or non-teaching, any student or parent ever told them of something they were learning or doing, they were always keen to hear about it.

These two men clearly demonstrated an open-minded zest to learn and grow, which permeated the whole organization. Learning was exciting and "cool" for the students, so they were all fully engaged. Certainly, as an adult, I was kept on my toes by their positive attitude and the positive challenges they presented to us!

Rather than focusing on problems, the Principal and Deputy-Principal both had resolved to create and foster an organization that was solutions-oriented. When issues arose at the School, the Principal and Deputy consciously resolved to see them not as problems but as opportunities. This gave them the space to see the issue, whatever it was, as an opportunity to discover a mutually beneficial resolution for all. It was even important to them to avoid using the word "problem."

There was one time when I saw the Deputy walk up to the Principal with a smile on his face and say, "Well…we appear to have another 'opportunity'!" The Principal smiled. This meant there was some student behavior, of a serious nature, to deal with. They both immediately walked calmly towards the situation, ready to give it their full attention and care.

In this solutions-based approach, the so-called "problem" was simply the catalyst for new opportunities and discovery. Their belief was that some new resolution, which no-one had thought of yet, was always possible. They both spoke often of how the one thing we all have absolute control over is our attitude. We can't completely control external circumstances, but our attitude is entirely up to us at every moment.

This approach applied to student behavior, school management at all levels, and matters relating to parents, teachers or the community as a whole.

This sounds all well and good in theory, and it's easier said than done if you're emotionally invested in focusing on the problem! Transforming our mindsets required a higher level of self-discipline. We had to put aside our own preferences, and commit to choosing the right attitude, a positive attitude, every time.

I consciously employed this approach when working with my own students and their parents. I began to see that it always resulted in amazing growth, love and respect as we resolved situations without judgment, and with full responsibility and ownership.

In time, it was clear to all that looking to the solution was the intelligent thing to do because just focusing on the problem changed nothing. They gave everyone a great example of the transformative power of a positive attitude: a constructive point of view, the intent that everyone benefit, and effective conduct that brought about productive results.

The Principal and Deputy's commitment to applying this approach in the school, allowed amazing engagement throughout the organization and boundless enthusiasm because no matter what happened, we could always learn and grow from it.

This is the transformative power of choosing a positive attitude.

Practices

Key Choosing Openness, Optimism, and Strength in Your Approach to the World and Yourself

Starter Count Your Blessings

One of the easiest and most powerful ways to shift our attitude is through gratitude. Gratitude is the natural state of the heart. So, let's begin to cultivate an attitude of gratitude by counting our blessings.

- Sit down somewhere quiet with a pen and your journal or some paper.

- Reflect on all the wonderful things in your life; reflect on your blessings. This could be as simple as the ground that supports each step you take. The air you have breathed freely today. The food you have eaten. The love of family, spouse, partner or friend. The support from your co-workers. The list is endless. Think "white paper" rather than "black dot."

- Write down your blessings. Be generous.

- Do this exercise of "Counting Your Blessings" every day for one week. Write down what you are grateful for each day.

After one week, you might like to extend this Starter Practice and continue to keep a Daily Gratitude Diary.

Intermediate Start the Day Right!

Part One:
- Upon waking, and as a matter of discipline, decide that you will have a positive attitude today no matter what! For example,
  - you could decide to praise your co-workers when you arrive at work.
  - You could resolve to treat any challenges as an opportunity to learn and grow.
  - You could say a prayer or positive affirmation such as "Today I see the world and myself as beautiful and healthy, and everything is in perfect order."

- Start the day decisively with a thought such as this, a thought that lifts your spirits. You are making a deliberate choice about your attitude for that day.

- Because it is a matter of discipline and not governed by any other factors, just do this even if you have doubts that it will work, or you don't feel like it, or you are convinced you can't do it. No "ifs" or "buts" or "reasons why," just do it anyway because it is a matter of discipline. Full stop! Period!

- Do this for one week. That's seven days. That's only seven times! Make a tick list if that helps and check off each time until you reach seven. Congratulate yourself when you've completed the seven days.

If you get up and forget to choose a positive attitude, that's not a problem. Do it as soon as you remember during the day. That still counts. It may take a few days before the memory wakes up when the body gets out of bed in the morning. Memory is like a muscle and sometimes it needs some training to get a bit stronger. Not a problem, be patient with yourself!

Part Two:
- After seven days, review. Note that we're reviewing after you've completed the seven-day practice.
  Warning: this review process is not so you can be self-critical. The point of the review is to gain new insights so, if necessary, you can resolve to change your attitude for the better.

- Review questions to ask yourself:
  - How do I normally start each day?
  - What is my usual attitude each day?
  - How does this usual attitude colour the rest of the day?
  - Am I aware of how my attitude is influencing and under-pinning my experience each and every day?
  - How do changing circumstances seem to affect my attitude and therefore my reactions to them?
  - What would happen if I were to consciously choose to adopt a positive attitude upon waking up each day?

- As you feel your attitude shifting and becoming more positive, reflect on how life has changed since becoming aware of your attitude:
  - What has each day been like with a conscious decision to have a positive attitude?
  - When I remember my attitude during the day what effect does that have?
  - What challenges have I faced in keeping a positive attitude?

Advanced The Whole World Is Your Teacher

The timeless wisdom traditions remind us regularly that our "teacher" is everywhere. Our teacher is always in front of us. Even when that doesn't seem to be the case there is always an opportunity to encounter your teacher and learn.

For example, an elite gymnastics coach once said: "The ground is your best teacher!" This means that we never lack for guidance, instruction and new knowledge. Some teachers are people; some teachers appear as experiences.

So, in the spirit of remembering that everyone and everything is our teacher:

- Pick a thing, a person or a circumstance in your life or your day, for which you find it hard to feel gratitude. If something or someone doesn't immediately spring to mind, don't rush this, give yourself time to consider.

- Then consciously find something to be grateful for in relation to this thing, circumstance or person. For example, you might like to ask yourself:
  - What am I learning from this situation or person?
  - What is the lesson that is tailored-made for me?
  - What am I grateful for in this blessing of a personal lesson?

Please remember that this is not an exercise in self-criticism, It is to raise aware ness and gain insight and to open up to the opportunities that are ever-present. It is only through this process that we grow, evolve and flourish.

We have now looked in some detail at the potency of our attitude, and the importance of a Positive Attitude, particularly one that is solutions oriented. However, many of us find ourselves in a situation where we feel locked in to an attitude to life that is anything but positive. In this state, suggestions such as feeling gratitude or using affirmations may not seem to work. Often this locked-in state is due to a feeling of being powerless in the face of external events and the people in our lives. This is a state of victimhood. We will address this key blockage—victimhood—in the next chapter and outline an effective method for moving from Victim to Victor. A key element in this move to freedom is the astonishing power of simply making a choice.

Chapter Seven

CHOICE, CHANGE, AND MOVING FROM VICTIM TO VICTOR

"A man who conquers himself is greater than one
who conquers a thousand men in battle."

—Buddha

In this chapter we are going to look at the move from Victim to Victor. We will look at how choice is a key factor, and how we are always free to choose. To emerge from the "culture of victimhood" we choose to be a victor instead. This is a solutions-based approach and a powerful proof that a change of attitude changes our lives.

For some with feelings of being at the mercy of external events and the people in our lives this may seem impossible. It isn't. For those who have been the victims of abuse, neglect or crime this may seem especially hard to face, but we can look to the timeless wisdom of Sanskrit to clarify the situation and open a pathway to real freedom and victory.

The following story from *The Odyssey*, an Ancient Greek epic, illustrates how resolve, creativity and taking ownership overcome an almost impossible situation. These qualities and Odysseus's choice to change his perspective and take action took him from being a victim to attaining victory.

Odysseus and Polyphemus, the One-eyed Cyclops

Odysseus, King of Ithaca, and his army of men were returning from their victory in the Trojan War. They sailed through the inky darkness of night and reached the shore of a lonely island. The inhabitants of this island were nowhere to be seen. Odysseus's men were hungry and tired, so, regardless of any lurking danger, they pulled into shore and disembarked. Before venturing further inland to explore the island, they settled down and refreshed themselves with a meal from the last of their supplies.

♦

Once satisfied, they prepared to discover what this land had to offer. Not far into their trek, they came upon a large cave. The cave was full of sheep and the walls were lined with shelves creaking under the weight of jugs of rich milk and piled high with cheese.

"Oh Ho!" cried one of Odysseus's men, "Let's grab as much of this as we can to replenish our stores."

"Yes," said another, "then let's get away from whomever lives in this cave and owns these sheep."

His men were agreed and began to gather food and herd the livestock towards the cave entrance.

Odysseus however was not in a rush to leave. He wanted to explore the cave. He wanted to see if there was anything else to be had in this rich storehouse. After all, there didn't seem to be anyone about, just some sheep in a pen, and this wonderful larder.

♦

So Odysseus and his men went further into the cave. After some time had passed, they heard the sounds of heavy footsteps approaching. They ran to the cave entrance and to their astonishment, they saw in the gathering sunset a one-eyed giant, a Cyclops, lumbering up the hill towards them. The Cyclops was herding more sheep before him.

There was no retreat! Odysseus and his men moved back into the cave to await their fate.

◆

The Cyclops drove his sheep into the cave and walked right past Odysseus and his men. Before they had time to slip out, the Cyclops turned to a huge boulder and rolled it across the entrance of the cave blocking any chance of escape. He lit several lamps and then herded his sheep into their pens. Odysseus and his men were sealed in for the night. They were trapped!

The Cyclops penned his sheep, removed his coat, placed some large jars of milk on a shelf. Suddenly he stopped. He sniffed the air and turned his single eye this way and that. He saw the mess that Odysseus's men had made of his stores.

"Well," he boomed, "I seem to have some visitors!"

Odysseus's men scattered to the corners of the cave, hiding behind any basket or jar that they could find.

However, Odysseus walked to the middle of the floor and waved a hand to get the giant's attention.

◆

"Greetings," he called.

The giant turned and peered into the gloom.

"Who is it who dares trespass in my cave?" he called. "What is your name?"

"My name is Nobody," Odysseus replied respectfully. "My men and I are wayfarers returning to our home, tossed to this island by the storms and seas. We have stopped here to rest and replenish our stores. We wandered into your cave and noticed your healthy sheep and delicious milk and cheese. May we beg you to spare some of your abundant stores and allow us to be on our way?"

◆

"Well, Mr. Nobody," the giant bellowed, "my name is Polyphemus. I am the son of Poseidon. You are thieves who have come to rob me of my goods. I know just how to deal with thieves!"

With that, Polyphemus swept his huge arm into the corner of the cave and grabbed two of Odysseus's men. He bashed their heads on the stone floor and ate them in one mouthful.

"Mmm delicious!" said Polyphemus, "I'm looking forward to eating the rest of you for my dinner this week. As a sign of my goodwill and hospitality, I shall eat you last, Mr. Nobody."

Polyphemus, continued to eat from his well-stocked shelves and drink wine until his belly was full, then he laid down and fell deeply asleep. The cave reverberated with his drunken snores.

The mood amongst the men was mutinous. They were trapped and helpless because Odysseus had wanted to explore the cave. Odysseus knew he had to come up with a plan. If they did nothing, they would be done for. He spent the night thinking hard about how to save the situation.

◆

In the morning the Cyclops awoke, rolled the boulder away from the cave's entrance and herded the sheep outside for their daily grazing. Before leaving, however, he rolled the enormous boulder back across the entrance, imprisoning Odysseus and his men.

"Find a wooden stake," Odysseus instructed his men as soon as Polyphemus was gone.

The men fanned out to all corners of the cave and soon returned with a long wooden pole.

◆

"Now sharpen the end," Odysseus instructed, "and hide the stake behind those baskets."

When this was done, he instructed his men to prepare food for the giant's dinner. Odysseus himself found a large jar of wine.

Odysseus and his men waited for Polyphemus to return. They were too anxious even to eat any of the rich provisions in the cave.

◆

At the end of the day they heard Polyphemus returning and then they saw the boulder being rolled to the side. Polyphemus's herds trotted into the cave followed by the giant himself. He immediately turned and rolled the boulder back into place, sealing the entrance.

"Welcome home!" Odysseus greeted their host. "You must be tired after your day's work. Let me serve you some wine. My men and I have prepared dinner for you. Please sit so we can serve you."

The ignorant Polyphemus was flattered and greedily drank several mugs of wine and ate plates of roasted meat that they had cooked. The huge quantity of wine and food made him feel drunk and drowsy, and before long he fell asleep in front of the fire.

◆

Odysseus's men raced to get the sharpened stake. They thrust it into the fire until the point was blazing hot. Odysseus and his men took up the red-hot stake and plunged it into the single eye of the Cyclops.

Polyphemus awoke shrieking.

"Polyphemus, what's wrong?" cried his neighbours, hearing the commotion.

"They are killing me!" he screamed out in agony.

"Who is killing you?" shouted his neighbours, readying themselves to come to his rescue.

◆

"Nobody!" shouted Polyphemus. "Nobody is killing me!"

When his neighbours heard that, they concluded that he was drunk and having a bad dream, so they all went back to bed.

The Cyclops groaned all night in pain.

◆

In the morning his sheep began bleating to be let out to graze. So, the giant staggered about the cave and eventually found his way to the entrance. He grasped the boulder with his huge hands and rolled it away from the entrance. In the meantime, Odysseus and his men had climbed under the sheep and each man clung to the woolly bellies. Polyphemus, hoping to prevent their escape, felt each sheep but he missed the men swinging below.

> Thus, Odysseus and his men escaped from the cave unseen by the blind Polyphemus. They were also able to carry many of Polyphemus's stores away with them.
>
> ◆
>
> Once safely on-board their ships again, and with their provisions restocked with milk, cheese, and many of Polyphemus's sheep, Odysseus and his men set sail.
>
> Polyphemus lumbered out of the cave and staggered down to the shore.
>
> "My name is Odysseus, King of Ithaca!" Odysseus called out to the blind Polyphemus.
>
> Polyphemus lifted his sightless face towards the sky and shouted to his father Poseidon, calling for revenge on Odysseus and all his men.
>
> ~ from *The Odyssey*, book 9, by Homer

This story illustrates Odysseus's refusal to adopt a victim mentality. He saw the problem, who could miss it, and immediately looked for solutions. He saw opportunities in the way Polyphemus ate and drank and fell asleep, and also in the way the giant sent his sheep out every day to graze. Even Polyphemus's single eye presented an opportunity. This rather harsh story is an allegory of intelligence overcoming animal brutality, and of reason helping to avoid the prison of victimhood.

Odysseus is a symbol of intelligent, resourceful leadership. He shows what a human being can do if he chooses to take responsibility for his actions and his life. The alternative is to think there is no way out of the problem and to give up without even trying. Often this is linked to feeling a victim of circumstances.

A state of victimhood is deeply paralyzing. Odysseus shows us what freedom from victimhood looks like. His determination to find a solution unlocked new and creative possibilities which would not have been evident if he had remained fixated on the problem. Throughout the *Odyssey*, an epic tale full of excitement and drama, Odysseus is constantly coming up with imaginative solutions to dire, seemingly impossible, situations. He had no rule book or guide, but he stepped up with a determination to succeed. Rather than a victim of circumstances he was a victor, who achieved ultimate success. He was able to return home safe despite the many challenges and dangers he and his men faced on their journey.

What Does Sanskrit Teach Us about the Meaning of Victim?

The Sanskrit for these two concepts is direct and uncompromising. A person locked into an attitude of victimhood is bound and tethered. They have effectively given their power away and have rendered themselves weak and impotent.

A victor, on the other hand, is a conqueror, is one who is free, in control and can choose any direction for their life.

Let's examine two Sanskrit words for "Victim":

Bali (बलि) means a sacrificial offering. Something that is offered in sacrifice to a higher power.

A sacrificial victim is a tribute or offering that is made in a ritual sacrifice. It is offered up to a higher power to benefit the one who makes the sacrifice. The word bali—victim—is derived from a root that carries the meaning of "suffering."

So, the first level of meaning for victimhood is something—either animate or inanimate—suffering and enduring through the act of being offered in sacrifice. The sacrifice benefits others, not the victim.

Yajña-pashu (यज्ञपशु) means a sacrificial animal.
"Yajña" means a sacrifice, and "pashu" is a tethered animal; figuratively "pashu" means a person ignorant of sacred things.

A yajña-pashu is a tethered sacrificial animal, not an inanimate object, but an animal that is tied up waiting to be offered in sacrifice.

While these images of animal sacrifice might seem grim to you, there is a positive aspect to the idea of sacrificing an animal. In the wisdom literature, animals often symbolize our lower nature. It is from here that our basic survival instincts arise such as eating, sleeping and reproducing. Our higher nature encompasses the power of reason, language and the ability to make an informed choice. Thus yajña-pashu can mean the sacrifice of our lower instincts in order to allow our higher nature to dominate.

When we are in the victim mindset, we are tethered and bound and imprisoned, waiting to be sacrificed for the benefit of the one who makes the sacrifice. The Sanskrit term "yajña-pashu" can be seen as a call for us to make a sacrifice and give up a victim mentality so we can become victors. This is not to say that people who have been victims of crime or abuse should not respond through the law, or through therapy or other practical and effective means of dealing with literal victimhood. The aim here is to use the wisdom of Sanskrit to identify the mental state of victimhood, its nature and effect, and then to find a pathway to healing and freedom so that we do not have to keep carrying the burden in our lives.

How does someone get into a state of victimhood? To be in a state of victimhood requires us to render ourselves powerless by surrendering our personal authority and creativity. The responsibility for our happiness and freedom of thought and action appears to be in the hands of others. For example, our power to change a situation in a fruitful and healthful way is sapped when we are angry, frustrated and feel powerless in the face of others who are dominant and pushy.

We have to be careful here. Most of us have experienced moments in our lives when people or events have been genuinely harsh or worse. Some have suffered abuse: physical or psychological.

What we are addressing is the difference between events, and the mindset that those events triggered. It is the mindset that perpetuates the state of victimhood, sometimes long after the events happened. What we are trying to do in this chapter, is lay out a path that, if followed, leads to mental and emotional freedom, a releasing of the burden and true healing.

To do this we need first to be honest and straight about what makes up the victim mentality, what are its essential features. Sanskrit speaks of a victim as being essentially powerless.

The characteristics of this state of victimhood are blaming others or circumstances, making excuses for inaction, and denial that we can take responsibility for our mindset and attitude. For example, some people use their lunchbreak at work every day to join their co-workers in bad-mouthing management's latest decision. This fetters people to a repetitive cycle of thoughts and speech. Nothing new, no benefit, change or freedom is possible in a state of victimhood.

Odysseus was the opposite, he took ownership of the situation, he accepted his accountability as leader of his men, and took responsibility for creative and effective action. In this way, he attained victory over the situation and freedom for his men and himself.

Let's move on and see what Sanskrit has to teach of the alternative perspective of being a Victor.

What Does Sanskrit Teach Us about the Meaning of Victor?

The Sanskrit meaning of "victor" is simple: you have won! There's no state of partial victory, if you win then you've won.

Jetā (जेता) A conqueror; victorious, triumphant.

The word for "victor" comes from the root "ji." This root means: to win, conquer, vanquish, excel, surpass, overcome, to be victorious.

Being a victor according to Pāṇini, involves both excelling and overcoming.

We excel in some field or undertaking, and we overcome any challenges or obstacles.

Internally, "excelling" means we connect with that in ourselves which is excellent: our goodness, our intelligence, our skills and talents. Internally, "conquering" means we overcome negative habits, distractions and obsessions. As victors, this leads to success and prosperity, and we can also be better friends, parents, colleagues, workers or bosses.

To be a conqueror and victor in life, is to take ownership of our own experience, to be accountable for our own decisions and to take responsibility for the outcomes.

Moving from Victim to Victor

Moving from Victim to Victor is the key change. To make this move we change from blame, excuses and denial (B.E.D.) and enter a world of ownership, accountability and responsibility (O.A.R.). The O.A.R. is a symbol of adopting a proactive attitude. You take up your oar, and row where you want to go. Rather than being impelled by the stream of habits and ideas that would keep us bound, keep us inactive in B.E.D.

When we're stuck in B.E.D., it seems like we have no choice; we appear fixed in a state of victimhood. The good news is we can choose to get out of this state. We can choose to take up our O.A.R. and row.

This is not about blaming the victim. The point of learning about victim and victor is so we have new knowledge and greater awareness of what is actually happening in both states. Only then can we make a change and move from one to the other.

A culture of victimhood is prevalent these days. This reinforces a fixed, bound and powerless state through perpetual blame and making excuses, followed by denial that we have any part to play in resolving the situation. Expecting someone else to change, while we do nothing about our own attitude and state, is a futile exercise.

Of course, sometimes injustices occur, and some response is necessary to restore harmony and balance. This restitution is not possible from the powerless state of victimhood. You must be in a state of empowerment through choosing O.A.R. for permanent restitution to occur.

Choice Is the Key

Choice, by definition, means there is another option. Choosing the state of victimhood is choosing a state where we appear to be bound, trapped and to have no choices. It means we see ourselves as having no power at all. Choosing to be a victor means we are taking responsibility, using our talents, skills and strengths to meet challenges and overcome them. Being a victor means we can achieve our dreams.

Why would we choose victimhood over being a victor? What's the payoff?

It's easier! It takes no effort to surrender our power and give up responsibility. It takes strength, effort and willpower to change, be accountable and take ownership. In B.E.D. we passively wait to be rescued. To get out of B.E.D., by contrast, we summon our own power and strength and call on any help available. Some of the ways of taking up our O.A.R. are: prayer, affirmations, journaling, vision boards, goal setting and finding a community of like-minded and motivated people.

The point of choice is where we shall look next. We will discover that there are always other options. We can always rise above the bound and powerless state of victimhood to be a victor; a winner.

Let's awaken and choose to get out of B.E.D.!

What Does Sanskrit Teach Us about Choice?

Sanskrit tells us that choosing, selecting one thing over another, is a form of honoring.

Varaṇa (वरण), means the act of choosing, selecting, honoring.

Choice, by definition, implies there are alternate possibilities. Whenever and wherever we engage in the act of choosing, we are selecting something that we prefer. Ideally this preference is for something that is inherently good.

Sanskrit also includes with the act of choosing and selecting, the element of "honoring." We honor that which we value, respect and love. So, when we make important choices, we honor the best and highest.

A key element in choosing wisely is to be conscious and awake when we make our choices. All too often, however, we are asleep and unaware of our so-called "choices," which are not choices at all, they are habitual, unconscious reactions. We don't in fact consider or honour that which is best or most valued. We can see how inefficient this can be when we are choosing material things like a house or a car. If we are asleep to our choices when selecting our thoughts and feelings, then these can become unconsidered knee-jerk reactions. Hence the hasty word and the hurtful phrase that slips out before we know it. Also, in that form of sleep we are unable to exercise the choice to stop repetitive negative thoughts that churn in our minds. This lack of real choice creates the life that we live, and affects us as an individual, and also everyone with whom we journey through life, our family, friends and community.

To move from victim to victor we have first to raise our awareness and create a space where we can make real, conscious choices. In that space, it is completely natural to choose a better way, a way of transformation, possibilities and fulfillment. It is only through increased self-awareness that our choices will honor the highest and best in everything.

A Decision to Walk Free

Nelson Mandela (1918—2013) was an anti-apartheid warrior, lifelong advocate for democracy and freedom for all, and the first black president of South Africa. He is an example of the transformative power of choice. He was jailed for engaging in violent direct action and became a man, after twenty-seven years, who chose to forgive and befriend his jailers. Mandela believed that all people in his homeland of South Africa should be free, and it was to this end that he dedicated his life.

As a young man, he joined the struggle against apartheid. He was a co-founder of the armed wing of the African National Congress and oversaw an extensive anti-government bombing campaign.

In 1963 he was tried for sabotage and faced a possible death penalty if convicted. In 1964 during the trial, he gave his "Speech from the Dock," in which he stated his ideal of a democratic and free country where everyone would live in harmony and equality. He said he was willing to give his life for this ideal.

He was sentenced to life imprisonment. Mandela's commitment to freedom for all remained unwavering despite his incarceration. He walked free, after twenty-seven years in prison, in February 1990.

Mandela continued his work for freedom by fully involving himself in official talks to end white minority rule. In 1993 Mandela jointly won the Nobel Peace Prize with the President of South Africa at the time, F.W. de Klerk. On April 27th, 1994, at the age of seventy-six, Mandela voted for the first time in his life. On May 10th, 1994, Nelson Mandela was inaugurated as South Africa's first democratically elected president. At his inauguration ceremony, amongst his invited guests, was his chief prison guard.

Nelson Mandela stands as an example of someone who, throughout his life, suffered at the hands of others, but chose not to enter a state of victimhood. He faced opposition with courage and determination. He never chose to accept the powerless status quo with an attitude of blame, excuses and denial. He maintained a belief that positive change was always possible and that he could contribute to that change.

Above all Nelson Mandela knew that if he didn't leave bitterness and hatred behind when he stepped out of prison, then he would never really walk free.

There is a lesson here for all of us. Nelson Mandela was a victim and must have naturally had times when he felt low. This is the same for all of us. Despite the challenging events of his life, he never lost sight of where his power lay, thus he chose to walk free not only from the physical prison but also from any state of victimhood.

Practices

Starter Creating the Space to Choose

This exercise need only take seconds; less than a minute.

- Take a moment, wherever you are and whenever you remember to stop what you are doing. Be sensible about where you do this! When you take a moment to stop, actually stop: physically, mentally and emotionally. Take a moment to pause the activity of life, you only need a moment.

- Now breathe in and out slowly and deeply once or twice.

- In the space that has opened up, choose what physical action you are going to do next. For this starter exercise, keep your deliberate choice to a physical action. Observe what you choose to do and how you choose.

- Repeat this starter exercise of creating the space to choose, several times each day for at least one week. Start to note if the quality of your choices changes. Have no expectations, just simply observe and take note.

- Stop – Pause – Breathe – Choose.

Intermediate Choosing Wisely

Take the exercise of Stop – Pause – Breathe – Choose further, by choosing your attitude wisely.

- Stop what you are doing. Pause for a moment.

- Breathe deeply and slowly once or twice. Observe without judgment, if you have unconsciously been in a prevailing attitude of "Staying in B.E.D." (Blame, Excuses and Denial)

- Have you been requiring others to change, or judging their words, or criticizing their actions?

- From this increased awareness, deliberately choose to make a change right now. Regardless of what is happening, choose to find a solution, choose to be positive, choose to be creative. Choose to pick up your O.A.R. (Ownership, Accountability and Responsibility) and start rowing! This takes practice, but you need to start sometime, so why not now?

- Stop – Pause – Breathe – Choose.

Advanced Wake-up, Get out of B.E.D., and Row with Your O.A.R.!

Take your experience of Stop – Pause – Breathe – Choose to the advanced level by resolving to change your victim mentality to a victor mentality. Remember that conscious choice has the quality of honoring the selection; choosing what's best.

- As often as you can manage during the day, create the space within yourself to choose.
    - Stop – Pause – Breathe – Choose.
    - Stop what you are doing and pause for a moment.
    - Take a slow deep breath in and out.
    - Let your mind and heart be still and calm.

- Now with a sense of honor to yourself, choose to be a victor today. Without judgment, ask yourself:
    - What is my attitude now?
    - Am I waiting for someone or something to change before I will?
    - Are my choices today honoring what is the best in others and myself?
    - Are my actions responding or reacting to the situation?
    - Have I been avoiding taking action out of blame, excuses or denial?
    - If my resolve is to be a victor, what could I do right now?

We have now looked in detail at the shift from victim to victor. The key is to make a choice to move out of the narrow world of blame, excuses and denial (B.E.D.) into the freedom and empowerment of ownership, accountability and responsibility (O.A.R.). Having made the choice to move, action is required. This action involves a systematic progression through The Seven Gateways of Transformation, and this is the subject of the next chapter.

Chapter Eight

THE SEVEN GATEWAYS OF TRANSFORMATION

"I shall now describe to you, O Rāma,
the seven states or planes of wisdom.
Knowing them you will not be caught in delusion:

Pure wish or intention is the first;
Enquiry is the second;
The third is when the mind becomes subtle;
Establishment in truth is the fourth;
Total freedom from attachment or bondage is the fifth;
The sixth is cessation of objectivity;
And the seventh is beyond all these."

—*Yoga, Vāsishta of Vālmīki*
(Book III, 118, 5 – 6)

The Seven Gateways to Transformation are based on the seven states or planes of wisdom of Vasishta. They are drawn from the wisdom literature of the East. They can be conceived of as levels, or steps, or indeed gateways of transformation and growth. Another way of thinking about these seven levels, is as a journey from a state of limitation to one of freedom as we further develop Conscious Confidence.

The City of Seven Gates

One day a man, wanting freedom, heard that he would find it in the City of Seven Gates. He set out on the road, looking for that wonderful city.

After searching for a long time, he came to a fertile valley. In that valley was a beautiful city surrounded by seven walls, each pierced by a single gate. He had found the City of Seven Gates.

At the First Gate he asked, "What must I do to pass through this Gate?"

♦

"You have already fulfilled the first task," said the Gatekeeper. "Having been told of the City of Seven Gates you set out to find it. Arriving here is the test of the First Gate."

The Seeker passed through the First Gate into the City. Beside the Second Gate was a school teacher.

"Kind Sir," the Seeker asked, "how may I pass through the Second Gate?"

♦

Without a word the Teacher pointed to a few loose piles of rubbish, some pots and pans and an old rug. Next to each were cleaning materials. There were others already at work.

The Seeker felt irritated. He wanted freedom and enlightenment, and he was being asked to perform menial tasks. One of the others already working noticed the Seeker and with a friendly wave summoned him to join the group. With this encouragement the Seeker was able to put his annoyance aside. He began to clean, at first half-heartedly, but by the time he had finished, his resistance had dropped away; he was enjoying the camaraderie of his fellow workers, he felt a sense of satisfaction and he was ready to do more. He turned to the Teacher who was smiling at him. The Second Gate had swung open unnoticed, and the Teacher was beckoning him and several others to pass through.

♦

At the Third Gate was a man with a sharp sword strapped to his waist.

"Tell me I pray," the Seeker said bowing low, "what must I do to pass through the Third Gate?"

The Gatekeeper told him a story: "The grandmother of two starving children stole bread to feed them. The punishment for stealing is ten copper coins or Gaol. The baker she stole from is also poor and his family depends on him selling his bread. The baker insists that the sentence be carried out as a warning to future thieves. To pass through the Third Gate you must render judgment in this case."

The Seeker was perplexed. Should he be merciful, and therefore flout the law and ruin the baker; or should he deliver justice and punish a desperate grandmother?

He pondered this for some time. His mind grew tired as he tried to figure a solution to this puzzle. Then he relaxed and stopped thinking, and his mind cleared. He saw the situation from another perspective. He understood that the Gatekeeper's sword was two-edged and stood for Reason and Love combined into one powerful force. The solution appeared before his very eyes.

"Here is my judgment," he said reaching into his own purse. "The fine must be paid. So here I make a gift of ten copper coins to the grandmother to pay the fine.

"I also decree that every person who knew the grandchildren were starving, but did nothing, must pay a fine of half a copper coin to the grandmother so she can, in future, pay the baker for her bread."

The Gatekeeper nodded. "It is the joining of head and heart, of reason and love that opens the Third Gate."

The Seeker passed through the Third Gate.

♦

The Seeker felt his confidence growing. With each step his fears and doubts faded away. Temptations to return to his old habits and leave his quest no longer had any power over him.

When the Seeker arrived at the Fourth Gate, he saw that it stood open already. Instead of a single Gatekeeper, there were men and women with their heads cocked as if listening to sounds coming from the inner city. They wrote down what they heard, and messengers took those notes to the outer city.

"What goes on here?" the Seeker asked.

"Listen," said one of the Scribes, who turned his head, as if listening to a sound carried on the breeze. "Can you hear it? Listen with your heart."

The Seeker fell silent and listened. After a few moments he began to hear a wonderful sound, like music, full of peace and insight and truth. The Scribe smiled and nodded and gave the Seeker paper and pen.

"Translate what you have heard into the language of the outer city."

The Seeker sat next to the other Scribes and he listened and wrote. He spent many happy days translating what he heard coming from the inner city, into art, poetry and laws for those in the outer city who wished to live a just and happy life. As time passed his hearing refined. A pathway opened within him until he no longer needed to listen with his ears. He began to hear the music coming from his own heart.

One day he knew it was time to go. He handed his pen to another Seeker who had just arrived from the Third Gate. Then he turned and passed through the Fourth Gate.

At the Fifth Gate the Seeker found an empty chair.

♦

He sat in the chair. Passers-by nodded and smiled at him. He watched people going about their business. Trees bent in the breeze, leaves fell softly to the ground.

The Seeker sat quietly and watched all of this. Then a cover gently fell from his heart. Love poured out of him. He saw each woman as his sister, his daughter, his mother, each man was his father, his brother, his son. All the children were his children. Everyone was part of one great family. His family.

He sat for some time in that simple chair next to the wooden gate swimming in an ocean of love. When the time was right the Seeker arose from his chair and walked through the Fifth Gate.

Next to the Sixth Gate was a ladder. The Seeker climbed the ladder and reached a platform. On it stood a woman. On her finger sat a songbird, trilling its greeting to the morning sun.

The Seeker looked around. He saw the woman, the bird, the rising sun, the city, everything shining in the golden light. Then he saw the light shining off everything as a single Light. He felt the beauty of everything as a single Beauty. Understanding flooded into his heart as a single Wisdom. Everything he looked at, everything he heard, everything he felt was One.

The woman smiled at him.

He climbed down the ladder and walked to the Sixth Gate. He stood and waited. At this gate there was nothing to do, no act to perform, nothing to say.

How long did he stand there? A moment? An eternity? Was it important? Not to him.

◆

Between one moment and the next the Sixth Gate opened, and the Seeker felt the invitation to walk through.

When he approached the Seventh Gate he began to laugh.

The Seventh Gate was a polished brass mirror. Etched into the mirror were the words: "Behold the Gatekeeper." All the Seeker could see was himself.

He bowed to his own reflection and stepped into the Seventh Gate.

~ a story by Gilbert Mane, based on his book: *7 Steps to Freedom*

—◆—

What Does Sanskrit Teach Us about These Seven Gateways?

The Seven Gateways can be seen as seven steps on the path to freedom, confidence and fulfillment. The Sanskrit word for each step holds deep and timeless wisdom that tells us the nature of each step and what is needed at each of the gateways. This sevenfold system sets out a natural step by step pathway from a world of fear and limitation to a world of Conscious Confidence and ultimate freedom.

The Seven Gateways are:

- Gate One: Inspiration or Good Impulse: Shubhechchā
- Gate Two: Application and True Enquiry: Suvichāranā
- Gate Three: Assimilation and Refinement of the Mind: Tanumānasā
- Gate Four: Illumination and a State of Clarity: Sattvāpatī
- Gate Five: Penetration with Insight and Detachment: Asangsaktī
- Gate Six: Dissolution and Non-Awareness of Separate Objects: Padārthabhāvanī
- Gate Seven: Completion in Full Realization of Unity: Turīya

These Seven Gateways to Transformation fall into two groups. The first three Gateways—Inspiration, Application, Assimilation—are the lower levels where we practice and refine. Here we follow wise directions from those trusted guides who have laid out pathways and practical exercises that work against our negative habits. The result is a gradual lightening and refinement of our being.

This process requires effort to hold to the disciplines laid down by the wisdom traditions and teachers. Persistent application of wisdom and guidance is needed because at this stage the main pitfall is that we fall back into old habits. It is these old, limiting habits that we need to replace. We continue to repeat this process of going through Gateways One, Two and Three until we are ready to move to Gateway Four.

Gateways Four, Five and Six form the second group. They are at a higher plain of consciousness and can seem difficult to get our heads around. The effort required at these higher levels is different. Here it is a letting go, a kind of "effortless" effort. The difference is between the effort of closing your hand to retain your grasp, and the effort required to let your fingers open of their own accord. Holding firm to the pathway and discipline of Levels One, Two and Three, gives way to letting go of any residual identifications and attachments at Levels Four, Five and Six.

The higher group of Four, Five and Six—Illumination, Penetration, Dissolution—is included here for the sake of completion, but the best way is to concentrate on the first three Gateways and let the higher levels take care of themselves, and they will, in due course. Gateways Four, Five and Six become available through the strength and clarity that has evolved in us through the disciplined effort and practice that we undertake at Gateways One, Two and Three.

The final level of Completion, Turiya, is limitless transcendence, described in a variety of ways in all wisdom literature from Plato to the Buddha, from Jesus to Krishna, from the monks of Mount Athos to the modern adepts who are available today to anyone seeking ultimate freedom.

Gate One: Inspiration or Good Impulse
Shubhechchā (शुभेच्छा)
Inspiration or Good Impulse is when we are struck by the wisdom of some new idea from a book, or hearing someone speak, and we experience a desire to attain what we have heard about.

In the story "The City of Seven Gates" the Seeker wanted true freedom and heard about this city of seven gates, where he could fulfil his desire. He was inspired to set out on his journey. To pass through the First Gate required him to take some action. The journey to the city itself was that action.

This inspiration for something new can happen at any level. Here is an example: my husband heard from his brother about a spiritual teacher which inspired him to take up a lifelong pursuit of self-realization. At another level, my husband and I heard about ballroom dancing and we were motivated to take it up. We have danced for many years now.

Almost everyone has had this experience of inspiration where mental and emotional bonds are broken, and we enter a new and greater world. Inspiration can strike at any time, it happens spontaneously. We do, however, need to keep refreshing the inspiration because the energy naturally wanes, and we can simply lose impetus and be distracted by something easier and more pleasurable.

Gate Two: Application and True Enquiry
Suvichāraṇā (सुविचारणा)

With this new impulse, inspiration and desire, we now want something greater and need new knowledge to attain it. Good energy gives us motivation. However, at this point, we still have the influence of our old habits. These may have been useful in the past, but they can't take us any further. Relying on our old thoughts, habits and knowledge will recreate the same results; it will be more of the same.

Thus, true enquiry is a rational investigation into a new way of living. You now need to discover what is required for this journey, including what limiting behavior and habits to address. At this level of enquiry and application of new knowledge, the mind and heart gradually change and refine as well. For example, in the story the Seeker is presented with simple physical cleaning tasks at the Second Gate. He is irritated by this work because he rates his goal of true freedom as far more elevated than these basic tasks. However, he doesn't allow his personal reactions to stop him from engaging with this work. This illustrates how he over-came some of his habitual limiting thought patterns and attitudes by accepting the indications of the guide at the gate, and by just doing what was presented to be done.

In the example of learning ballroom dancing, after we were inspired to take it up, we had to find a dance teacher and then take regular lessons and do some practice. Our teacher required us to do things we hadn't done before. The lessons were mostly fun, but sometimes they were quite challenging. It was similar with the work my husband had to do in the initial stages of his spiritual journey.

In all these examples, the presence of a guide, teacher or mentor, and the company of like-minded people who can accompany us on our journey, is important to help refresh our resolve, remind us of our initial inspiration, and help guard and support us against falling into old habits that we want to shed.

This stage of enquiry and the application of new knowledge and guidance is crucial to any change and transformation. Without concerted effort, and diligent and assiduous practice of new knowledge, no transformation will occur, and old habits will reappear. Think of your last New Year's Resolutions.

Gate Three: Assimilation and Refinement of the Mind

Tanumānasā (तनुमानसा)

This Sanskrit word literally means "attenuation of the mind." To attenuate means to make something thinner or slimmer. Attenuation or the trimming of the mind occurs when the mind is under discipline and is being "starved" of its regular diet of negative thoughts and feelings. A refinement of the mind occurs at this stage because the new knowledge is applied continuously and is becoming assimilated. There is greater access to Reason rather than relying on habitual patterns of thinking. Old mental and emotional clutter is transcended, and a feeling of lightness, efficiency and strength grows.

In the story, the Seeker is required to make a judgement call. His old ways of thinking are of no use to him. He has to put them aside and allow both Reason and Love to operate together. In our ballroom dancing journey, there came a point where we had to let go of our thinking and allow the dancing itself to take over. This took our dancing to another level of proficiency and enjoyment. My husband spoke about a stage in his meditation practice where the thinking and the effort to focus fell away, and he was able to listen more easily to his mantra and follow it wherever it took him.

The first three Gateways—Inspiration, Application and Assimilation—require the support of guidance, practice and good company. This support helps us to keep on track as the mind and heart strengthen and refine, and also to help us avoid falling back into old habits.

The aim of this process of the first group—Gateways One, Two and Three—is to refine the mind and heart and to evolve good and healthy habits. This helps to establish a firm platform of confidence and strength within ourselves which is one of the main characteristics of Gateway Four: Illumination and a State of Clarity. Gate Four is the first Gateway of the second group: Gateways Four, Five and Six.

Gate Four: Illumination and a State of Clarity

Sattvāpati (सत्त्वापती)

This is a stage of stability, strength and lightness that is lacking in the previous three Gateways. At this point of illumination and in this state of clarity, fear falls away. Habits of the ego are clearly seen to be destructive and are easily avoided, with little apparent effort.

Gateway Four is attained because our being has refined, fear has fallen away and we feel confident, strong and steady. One effect of all this is an openness, receptivity and clearer understanding of what the wisdom traditions are saying. At the same time, we can use our experience of life to formulate that wisdom for others who are seeking guidance. This Gateway is a firm platform from which we are unlikely to fall back, because there is an established strength to stand on our own two feet. This is the first stage of Conscious Confidence.

In the story, the Seeker feels strong and fearless. He joins others at the Fourth Gate listening to the messages from the higher levels and translating them into a language that those at the outer gates can understand and follow. As our ballroom dancing progressed, this is the level, at which we were happy to say, that we were reasonably accomplished ballroom dancers who could walk out onto a dance floor and dance confidently with expression, and some established level of proficiency and artistry. My husband's spiritual journey became steady and clear, and he felt confident to pass on what he had learnt and discovered in practice to others seeking to follow the same path.

There are higher levels if we desire to go further. The work to be done is far more refined now. It is based on surrender and requires a shift in the type of effort to be applied. The effort needed here is the type used to unclench our fist rather than the effort needed to keep it closed.

The reason a consideration of the Seven Gateways appears here in the book is because of our need to move up from Victimhood to Victory. This involves exercising Choice and accomplishing real Change. The mechanism for achieving this is in the first three Gateways: Inspiration, Application, and Illumination. When we reach Gateway Four—Illumination—we have achieved the state of Conscious Confidence.

Thus, a detailed consideration of the higher Gateways: Penetration, Dissolution and Completion that are essentially concerned with levels of higher consciousness can be left for another day. Here it is sufficient to give a brief outline of the nature of each of these higher Gateways.

Gate Five: Penetration with Insight and Detachment
Asangsaktī (असंसक्ति)
At Asangsaktī we develop the power of detachment that penetrates all the different names and forms of everything we encounter. We have far

greater insight to see beyond the appearances of things, and to know that the source of everything is pure undivided consciousness. The usual operations of the mind, the chatter, the circling thoughts become quiet at this level.

Gateway Five—Penetration with Insight and Detachment—is not governed by the mind as we ordinarily know it. This is where reason and love operate in silence. It is at this stage that we, like the Seeker in our story, experience an outpouring of love and we see the whole world and everyone in it as our family. This is genuine and abiding. It doesn't come and go depending on circumstances.

Gate Six: Dissolution and Non-Awareness of Separate Objects
Padārthabhāvanī (पदार्थभावनी)

Padārthabhāvanī is characterized by a dissolution of separation. We still have a sense of an individual feeling of existence, and yet we perceive everything as a single blissful unity. We see no differences between all the manifold forms, creatures and beings. In the story the Seeker saw all light as one Light, all knowledge as one Wisdom and finally everything as the One.

At this stage all personal effort has fallen away. There is complete surrender.

Gate Seven: Completion in Full Realization of Unity
Turīya (तुरीय)

At this point, at Gateway Seven, words and descriptions are difficult. This is the stage of self-realization, satori, samādhi, enlightenment. Each tradition has its own way of describing the indescribable. Plato calls it the colourless, formless intangible essence. The *Katha Upanishad* says: "Eye, tongue cannot approach it, nor mind know.… It lies beyond the known, beyond the unknown."

It is said that none of our powers and efforts work to gain this level, that entry into this Gateway is, as it were, by invitation only. In our story the Seeker was content to wait, and when the door opened, he saw only himself and entered the Seventh Gate.

These Seven Gateways to Transformation describe the journey of the individual. The work we do in particular at the first three—Inspiration,

Application, Assimilation—is where we begin to experience the growing, liberating power of Conscious Confidence. At Gateway Four, Illumination, we achieve a stable and strong platform where Conscious Confidence is a natural part of our life and we experience ease, clarity and success.

The final three Gateways—Penetration, Dissolution and Completion—are further stages on a spiritual journey to ultimate enlightenment.

Unexpected Teachers

I have known a lady for many years. We have a common bond through our lifelong spiritual journeys. We studied the same timeless wisdom and we both practiced meditation every day for decades. This lady had been fully engaged with working at Gateways One, Two and Three of the Seven Gateways for decades.

A few years ago, she contacted me and said she was going to be in town visiting family. We hadn't seen each other for some time but she said something told her she needed to see me. We arranged a place and a time and met as planned. In the course of the conversation, she told me about an incident that had taken place a few weeks before.

She had heard of a spiritual teacher that was holding a public meeting in her hometown. She wasn't sure if she really needed to go, but she was concerned not to miss something important. So, she made arrangements to attend after work.

On the appointed day, she was delayed leaving work. Time was tight to catch the only bus that was going to get her there on time. It was raining and she had heavy bags. As she ran across the road to catch the bus, she tripped and fell in the middle of the street.

Her bags and belongings flew everywhere; she was lying on a busy road in the rain. A truck came to a sudden stop in front of her, the driver glared at her through the windshield.

She got to her feet and gathered her things; then she limped to the side of the road nursing a grazed knee and hand. She was shaken by the incident, but despite everything she still caught the bus and went to the meeting.

She enjoyed the gathering with the spiritual teacher, but she didn't find any extraordinary moments of enlightenment, it was just a pleasant evening.

As I listened to the story, what stood out for me was the moment when the truck driver glared at her as she lay on the wet road. I asked her what she knew in that moment of looking into the truck driver's eyes? What was the lesson?

"This is why I knew we needed to meet!" she exclaimed. "Now I know what I had to learn from the whole scenario."

The meaning of the evening's events was now plain to her. She realized that everyone and everything was her teacher. The road and the truck driver were her teachers. The rain was her teacher. Even running late was her teacher!

The specific lesson that she learnt, and which changed her whole approach to spiritual work, was that she didn't need to go to some special place and sit in front of a specific guru anymore. The teacher was always in front of her. She realized that those teachers had always been there, but now she had reached a stage where she had eyes to see and ears to hear. This gave her immense confidence. She knew that she had reached a level of strength, power and certainty, and that whenever she needed guidance it would be available.

I heard a quality of humility in her account of this revelation. She became blissful as her understanding deepened. She told me that she now felt grateful for tripping on the road and for the truck driver stopping suddenly before her. She experienced unity and love for all the elements of the scenario. This is a good example of having a strong and stable platform of Conscious Confidence at Gateway Four: Illumination and a State of Clarity.

The Power of Practice to Achieve Conscious Confidence

We have looked closely at the Seven Gateways of Transformation. We did this because we need to move from Victim to Victor and the Seven Gateways help explain the process of transformation. To make this move we need to consciously choose to get out of B.E.D.—blame, excuses and denial—and take hold of our O.A.R.—ownership, accountability and responsibility.

We need help and support because habit and our ordinary circumstances usually conspire against any such fundamental change. This help comes in the form of a series of practical steps that have been tried and tested and have proved effective in creating transformation from Victim to Victor. The F.U.S.E. Program is just such a system.

As we have seen, the work is done mainly at the first three Gateways: Inspiration, where we hear something new; Application, where we work at applying it; and Assimilation, where it has the effect of freeing our mind and heart of old habits. We repeat this until we attain a level of Conscious Confidence at Gateway Four: Illumination.

This leaves the higher Gateways of Five, Six and Seven—Penetration, Dissolution and Completion—for those who want to go further on the path of spiritual transformation. These higher levels require practices of a different nature, where the work is to let go, to surrender the effort.

For the purposes of developing Conscious Confidence, the practical exercises are focused on the first three Gateways.

Practicing is essential. It is like a muscle that needs training and strengthening. Practice requires hearing new knowledge and then faithfully applying it in daily life. This is how we discover the real meaning of that new knowledge for ourselves. Once information has been transformed into understanding, no one can take that understanding away from us.

To be consistent in applying what you learn on the journey of the Seven Gateways, remember that there are three different time factors involved with practice:

- The number of times that you practice each day (frequency)
- The length of time each practice lasts (duration)
- The period of days, weeks or even years, over which you keep practicing (extent)

It is over all these types of time—frequency, duration and extent—that theory is alchemized into experience.

Our attention needs to be on regular practice at Gateways One, Two and Three. If we faithfully do the work there, the higher levels of the seven steps will take care of themselves. I can promise you that!

The Four-Fold Energy of Conscious Confidence

In the Seven Gateways to Transformation, we learned how to move through the first three levels—Inspiration, Application and Assimilation —

until we develop the strength to attain Conscious Confidence at level four, Illumination. My practical F.U.S.E. Program is the means to build strength at levels one, two and three, and to attain to level four. The first two parts of the F.U.S.E. Program were set out in Chapter Five: Core Values, and Chapter Six: Positive Attitude. Core Values and a Positive Attitude are the fundamentals of the program. Based on these fundamentals, the F.U.S.E. Program now continues with the Four-Fold Energy of Conscious Confidence.

Sanskrit has many words for "confidence." Having studied and analyzed these Sanskrit words, I have synthesized their meanings under four headings. Each of these four groups has its own characteristic energy: Focusing, Uniting, Simplifying, and Energizing. This is the Four-Fold Energy of Conscious Confidence:

- **Focusing**:The characteristic energy of focusing is decisive, courageous, steady
- **Uniting:** The characteristic energy of uniting is compassionate, loving, supportive
- **Simplifying:** The characteristic energy of simplifying is straight, pure, true
- **Energizing:** The characteristic energy of energizing is dynamic, creative, enthusiastic

These four energies—Focusing, Uniting, Simplifying, Energizing—form the final sequence of the six-part F.U.S.E. Program. Once we have our Core Values and Positive Attitude, we move on to Focusing, then Uniting and Simplifying, and we round off the process with Energizing. I have laid out practical exercises to bring each step to life and to make it a matter of experience for you. The Key Practice is the theme of the specific practices that follow.

Chapter Nine

FOCUSING

"Concentration is the essence of all knowledge;
nothing can be done without it."

—Swami Vivekananda

"Concentration is the secret of strength."

—Ralph Waldo Emerson

In this chapter we are going to look at Focusing. "Focusing" is that power and ability to take our consciousness and concentrate it on one thing, whether it is an action like driving, or a thought, or even a feeling. This power to give focused attention implies the ability to let go of anything that would distract us. So focused attention is an act of giving. When our attention is whipped away by passing fancies it is being stolen. Our exploration of focused attention will be underpinned by looking at what Sanskrit tells us of: firm confidence, calm faith and conviction, all of which require Focusing.

The following story is of a warrior who mastered focused attention.

Arjuna and the Bird

Drona, the master teacher of the Pandava royal family, wished to test the princes. He made a bird out of straw and painted an eye on the face. He then placed it high in a tree.

"Take up your bows quickly," said Drona to the princes. "Fix your arrows and aim at the straw bird. As soon as I give the order, shoot at the bird's head."

First, he called Yudhishthira, the oldest of the Pandava princes.

"What do you see?" he asked.

"I see the bird, the tree, you and my brothers," said Yudhishthira.

"Stand aside," said Drona crossly.

One by one he called on all the princes. They all said the same as Yudhishthira. Drona was very angry. Finally, he called Arjuna.

Arjuna was forever grateful for the wisdom imparted to him by his great teacher Drona. He had absolute faith in his teaching. Arjuna was intent on excellence; he practiced regularly and was always inquiring about how to remain single-pointed throughout his training.

"What do you see?" Drona asked Arjuna.

"I see only the bird," said Arjuna.

"Describe the bird," said Drona.

"I can't," said Arjuna.

"Why not?" asked Drona.

"I can only see the eye," said Arjuna.

"Shoot!" said Drona. The head of the straw bird fell, pierced by Arjuna's arrow.

Arjuna had learnt the lesson of single-pointed attention.

◆

On another occasion Drona was swimming in the river when a crocodile caught his leg. Although he could have freed himself, he called for help. Arjuna pierced the crocodile with five sharp arrows while everyone else stood helpless.

Arjuna, through his unwavering respect for his teacher's instruction, and his diligent practice, had mastered attention. Drona thought of Arjuna as his best student and gave him the secret of many mighty weapons.

~ a story from the *Mahābharata*

Arjuna stands for the power to give our complete attention to something. This is a power that, with practice, we can all develop. Drona symbolizes our guide or teacher. The bird represents any worthwhile goal. The crocodile stands for the challenges and dangers we sometimes face in life.

It is when these times of challenge appear that we need focused attention the most. However, when this Fear Shadow descends, and in the midst of stress, or when we are under pressure, we often find ourselves distracted and unsteady. Maintaining our focus is the first of the four energies that help us to achieve Conscious Confidence.

Focusing is the power to give undistracted attention. The timeless wisdom of Sanskrit tells us that if we have firm confidence, calm faith and conviction then we will have that power and be able to control where our attention goes. Arjuna was decisive, courageous and steady. He had firm confidence, faith in his teacher, and the conviction that he would hit the target, and therefore he had supreme focus.

What Does Sanskrit Teach Us about Focusing?

There are three Sanskrit words for "confidence" that can help us understand the decisive, courageous and steady energy of Focusing. The first deals with firm confidence. The second speaks of calm faith. The third deals with conviction. Let's look into each of these three Sanskrit words and their deeper meanings.

The first of these words **dridha-pratyaya** (दृढप्रत्यय), means firm confidence, belief and assurance.

Pāṇini tells us that "firm confidence, belief and assurance" will be discovered in the experience of "growth, prosperity and happiness." Therefore, we need to look more closely at "growth, prosperity and happiness" in order to come to an understanding of dridha-pratyaya: firm confidence, belief and assurance.

So, the first question is: what does growth, prosperity and happiness look and feel like? The key feature is that they allow us to step into a larger world and live a freer more powerful life. I will concentrate on inner growth, prosperity and happiness because this will lead naturally to the experience of these qualities in the outer world as well.

The second question is: how do we cultivate the experience of inner growth, prosperity and happiness? The wise tell us that cultivating a positive approach to life, and positive emotions leads to this expansion of growth, prosperity and happiness. For example, the Buddha said of generosity: "Happiness never decreases by being shared." The Tao Te Ching says: "The heart that gives, gathers." There are many examples of wise teachers telling us that if we cultivate positive emotions and values, then our lives will be happier, more prosperous and we will experience growth.

The advice therefore is to cultivate positive feelings, emotions, attitudes and values like, for example: generosity, compassion, courage, happiness or love. Choose any positive emotion for which you have an affinity. You may wish to revisit the gratitude exercise in Chapter Six when you practiced Counting Your Blessings. Notice how a conscious effort to cultivate positive emotions leads to growth, prosperity and happiness, and not just for yourself but for those around you.

Pāṇini tells us that this experience of inner growth, prosperity and happiness will deepen our understanding of dridha-pratyaya: firm confidence, belief and assurance, which is the first aspect of Focusing.

The second Sanskrit word is **shraddhā** (श्रद्धा) meaning "calm faith, trust and respect."

Pāṇini tells us that calm faith, trust, and respect is nurtured by "holding our attention on the truth in our heart." This requires focused attention. The simplest way to hold our attention on the truth in our heart is to be still, centered and self-aware. This will nurture calm faith, trust and respect. There are practices at the end of this chapter such as The Witness, that will help you to be still, centered, and self-aware.

The third Sanskrit word is **nishchaya** (निश्चय) meaning "conviction, certainty and positivity."

Pāṇini's indication for nishchaya, is that "conviction, certainty and positivity" is found by "seeking, focusing and being intent upon higher knowledge." Lower knowledge is the information brought to us daily by our senses and our ordinary thinking processes. It is the knowledge of ordinary life. Higher knowledge is the conscious knowledge of underlying causes accessed through calm stillness and focused attention.

By seeking and being intent upon this higher knowledge, we gain conviction and certainty in the underlying lawfulness of the universe. This is often accompanied by an "Ah-ha" moment that has an emotional impact and naturally engenders a positive attitude. Notice that we are not asked to acquire higher knowledge. Sometimes, if we acquire our objective, we make no further enquiries. We only need to seek higher knowledge and remain focused and intent on it so that we may continue to grow and evolve.

The following story illustrates how acquiring too much knowledge can block the process of enquiry.

— ♦ —

More Tea?

A highly educated man, proud of his learning, went to visit a famous Zen master. The man talked unceasingly about Zen while the master quietly served tea.

The master poured the man's cup to the brim, and then kept pouring. The cup began to overflow. The learned man watched until he could restrain himself no longer.

"What are you doing?" the man exclaimed. "No more will go in! The cup is full!"

"As are you," the master calmly replied. "How can I teach you Zen if you don't first become an empty cup?"

— ♦ —

Arjuna demonstrated the three aspects of Focusing in the story of the straw bird. He had firm confidence in his skill and training, calm faith in his teacher, and simple conviction that he would hit the target. He had the power of attention.

Attention is another way of saying "focused consciousness." Attention is either given to something as you focus on it, or it is stolen away. Notice that when we talk about attention, we often say we are "giving" attention to something. When we are awake and in control, then our attention is freely given. It is an act of generosity.

Giving is like a "donation." The best donations are those that are given with no thought of receiving anything in return. When we make a donation to charity, we don't expect a reciprocal payment. When we donate, we give from the heart, without conditions.

So, when we focus our consciousness, we are giving or donating our attention. However, when we are in an ordinary state of awareness our attention is often stolen away by passing fancies or shiny objects. We see snakes where only ropes exist, and our attention is captured by fear, negativity and criticism.

Attention is like the life-giving sap flowing through a great tree, giving life to every branch and leaf. This is how the tree grows strong. If the sap stops flowing the tree dies. Our attention is going to something every moment of the day, whether we're aware of it or not.

Whatever our attention goes to grows. That's why giving attention is so powerful.

Choose wisely where your attention goes!

A Fear of Missing Out

A young woman, 23 years old at the time, came to me asking for help. Let's call her "Chloe." She lived in one of the major cities on the east coast of Australia, and she worked in an insurance company. She was single but had a supportive circle of friends and family. She was healthy, intelligent and capable. She had everything to look forward to.

What was her problem?

Chloe was feeling stressed, uncertain and unfulfilled. She had no clarity in herself or her life and felt unmotivated.

A friend who had consulted me in the past, had recommended to Chloe that she hire me as a coach. At first Chloe was not hugely enthusiastic to ring me but then thought, Why not? What have I got to lose?

In our initial phone call Chloe described much of what I have outlined above, and I realized I had to meet her face to face to get a true sense of her situation.

When we met at my consulting room what I saw was an apparently confident young woman who couldn't seem to keep her hands and eyes from her smartphone. When I asked her about it, she told me that she spent a lot of time every day on her phone; swiping the screen repeatedly, flicking from one image to another. She wasn't able to give me an estimate of how many hours, but I would guess that it was a lot. This behavior started in high school and had soon become a habit.

I asked what was keeping her so dependent on her phone, and she said that she needed to remain connected to friends and what was happening. When I asked her what would happen if she lost her phone, she looked panicky and was unable to give me a coherent reply.

It certainly seemed to me that Chloe felt she was connecting to some form of reality, but I was not so sure that it existed anywhere outside her own imagination. She did have real friends, of course, but the constant reference to a small glowing screen with images and text flashing by seemed a substitute for life, not real living.

So, I asked her to try one or two things.

First, I asked her to bring her awareness to her body and senses. She began to feel the energy that was running through her body.

Then I asked her to become aware of her feelings rather than her thoughts. Gradually, with a little guidance, she became aware of what was motivating her behavior. It was a fear that she would become disconnected if she didn't keep "checking in" with everything and everyone all the time. It was FOMO, "fear of missing out."

What Chloe needed was focus. Her mind was all over the place and she needed to gain the ability and strength to give her attention.

So, I asked her to look out of the window at a tree for a minute. Very quickly she became bored, and then she felt anxiety rising in her. She wanted to get back to her comfort zone of repeated stimulation and distraction. Tension and stress increased until she became irritated and agitated.

However, Chloe was intelligent and could see for herself that if being asked to look at a tree for a minute caused such a reaction, she needed my help. Her self-awareness of this reactive situation was an important first step. Her willingness to learn and engage was key.

What she needed most of all was to connect with reality in the here and now. No discussion or analysis - just direct experience. So, I took her through a practice of guided awareness. This time she felt some relief straight away; a calming peace washed over her. A new vitality, energy and enthusiasm arose within her. It felt so good, so inspiring and empowering that she wanted more. She agreed to try this practice for a week and to come back to see me again.

When she returned, she reported the following: Several times during the week it had come to mind to practice. Mostly she did so, but sometimes she ignored the reminder. There was usually something else tugging at her attention.

Even when she did practice, she found an insistent voice trying to get her attention. This voice was saying: "Just check-in quickly to see what's happening, it'll only take a moment," "Quick, I'm missing out," "I can be aware anytime, I'll do it in a moment, once I've looked at my phone," "Twenty emails, chats and messages must have come in while I've been sitting here doing nothing."

So, Chloe's next big step was to strengthen her "inner" muscles of determination when the alluring voice of habit spoke. To do this she needed an emotional anchor.

I asked her what she was grateful for. She started slowly, but eventually the words tumbled out: her family, her friends, her health and so on. Then I asked her to embrace that feeling and apply it to everything in her life. She began to cultivate an attitude of gratitude which brought a remarkable transformation in her outlook. She spoke of feeling so much larger and stronger simply through saying "thank you" throughout the day. She even said "thank you" to challenges, because she began to see these less pleasant events were helping her to grow.

She continued with regular moments of stillness and awareness, which developed her faith and trust in herself, and respect for her own beautiful qualities and talents.

She kept a gratitude diary, faithfully practiced stillness and awareness, and developed a conviction in the higher truth and power of herself. The strength she derived from these simple exercises, gave her a new and positive outlook that she didn't previously realize was possible. Her persistence opened up new dimensions of self-awareness.

Chloe set exciting goals for herself. She had a new-found motivation and focus. Now she knew what she wanted to do and had the energy, passion and confidence to pursue her dreams and live boldly. Through focusing and through gratitude, her faith and conviction grew, and she had become decisive, courageous and steady.

Practices

Key Giving Undistracted Attention

Starter One Task Magic

Give full attention to one simple task every day for a week.

- Choose a simple task and give your full attention to it. For example, washing your hands: Feel the water on your hands, feel your hands touching each other, listen to the sound of the water, watch your hands as they move, smell the soap, etc.

- The practice is to stay present in the moment as the task is performed by the body.

- Gently bring the attention back from any mental commentaries or emotional experiences. These may occur but let them come and go. The observation is the important part of this practice.

Intermediate Self-Investment

Part One: Reflection

Each day invest in your inner growth and inner prosperity.

Reflect each night before sleep: Have I invested in my inner growth, prosperity and happiness today? How can I invest a little more tomorrow?

This self-investment can take any form that appeals to you. You may find that classic spiritual literature such as the *Bhagavad Gītā* or the *Bible* appeals to you. There are many other books, both contemporary and traditional, about higher consciousness that may also inspire you. These works are readily available in accessible forms: books, e-books, podcasts and so on. You may find some contemporary teachers available to you in seminars, workshops, lectures or courses. Any of these are ways of investing in your inner growth.

One way to invest in your own development is to practice exercises such as The Witness, below, every day.

Part Two: The Witness

Stillness and Awareness: Spend a few minutes each day being still and aware.

- Sit quietly, relax, breathe and let your awareness open and expand.
- Be aware of the body.
- Watch the thoughts and feelings and let them come and go. There is no right or wrong experience. Witnessing is the key.

It's more effective to practice for a shorter period of time more often, rather than one longer period of time less frequently. Aim for two to three minutes each time you practice and aim to practice this exercise two or three times each day. Once you have practiced this "Witness" exercise a few times, and you can feel you are clearer, stronger and steadier, then write down all your strengths, talents and abilities.

The aim of this exercise is for you to acknowledge the best of yourself in the light of conscious self-awareness.

- What comes easily and naturally to you?
- What are you good at?
- What can you do that makes you feel happy and your heart sing?

Advanced Seeking Higher Knowledge

This is an exercise in seeking and being intent upon higher knowledge, and then acting on it. It is adapted from the *Taittirīya Upanishad*.

- In a situation where you don't know what to do, either in a specific case, or in a general way, or when you simply want some guidance and advice, then ask yourself: "What would a wise man or woman do here?"

- If a spontaneous and helpful answer appears, then follow its promptings.

- If your mind remains blank, then think of someone specific who is wise in the circumstances that you find yourself—another parent, a friend, a professional, a craftsperson—and ask yourself: "What would that specific person do in these circumstances?"

- Again, follow the promptings of whatever answer makes itself known. Discover the power of this question to lay out a path to higher knowledge. The key is to act on that knowledge.

This exercise is similar to The Flashlight exercise in Chapter Four, except here we ask about "doing" rather than "thinking."

Now that we have seen the importance of Focusing and have engaged in simple practices that help us to focus our attention, we can move to the next part of F.U.S.E. Program. This is Uniting, where we discover the power of compassion and love to bring people and things together.

Chapter Ten

UNITING

"Those who experience the unity of life see themselves
in all beings, and all beings in themselves, and look on
everything with an unprejudiced eye."

—*Bhagavad Gītā* 6,13

In this chapter we are going to look at Uniting, the next element of the
F.U.S.E. Program. "Uniting" is the power to see that which binds us all
together. The characteristic energy of Uniting is compassionate, loving
and supportive. It builds trust and confidence in families, communities and nations. Inner unity is the fruit of faith and belief in ourselves
through self-awareness. If we experience inner unity, we will see it everywhere we look.

The following story illustrates the power of unity and the weakness of
division.

Strength in Unity

A father had three sons. The eldest son was skilled in sport and
physical activities. He was very proud of his own strength and
abilities.

The middle son enjoyed studying and intellectual pursuits.
He excelled in his exams and thought he was much smarter and
superior than his brothers.

The youngest son was artistic and sensitive. He created beautiful artworks and wrote profound and inspiring poetry. Despite
this, he always felt that he was treated unfairly, and that no

one understood him, and that his father didn't stand up for him against his brothers; he often felt hard done by and sorry for himself.

Despite their natural abilities and talents, and much to the despair of their father, the three boys quarreled all the time. The father could see that if they didn't learn to live together harmoniously, someone could easily take advantage of one or all of them; that their disunity and divisive behaviour left them weak and vulnerable.

The father tried many times to tell them that they had to stop fighting and to get on with each other, but they ignored him. He was at his wits' end.

Then he had an idea.

◆

He went and collected a bundle of sticks and tied them firmly together. He called his sons out into the back yard.

He asked the first son to take the bundle of sticks and break them. The eldest son bragged to his father and two brothers that this was too easy for him as he was so strong and fit from his sport and training. He tried several times but was unable to break the bundle of sticks. He reluctantly gave the bundle of sticks back to his father.

Then the middle son stepped forward and took hold of the bundle of sticks. He smugly thought that he was clever enough to work out how to break it; that it took brains rather than brute strength. He also tried and tried without success. None of his clever strategies succeeded.

Finally, the youngest son took the bundle of sticks. He also thought that he could easily break it. After several attempts he gave up with a sulk, saying it was unfair and how could his father expect him to break the sticks.

◆

Then their father untied the bundle and handed his eldest son one of the sticks and asked him to break that. He was able to snap it easily.

Similarly, the second son broke a single stick immediately, as did the third son when it was his turn.

The three brothers, holding the broken sticks in their hands, looked at each other sheepishly. Then one by one they began to smile, and finally they began to laugh.

They threw the sticks on the ground and embraced each other in a way they hadn't for many a long year. Then they opened the circle and beckoned to their father to join the embrace.

They had learnt the lesson.

Unbreakable strength is in unity.

~ A traditional Panchatantra story

What Does Sanskrit Teach Us about Uniting?

There are two beautiful Sanskrit words that speak of inner connection and self-awareness, and of bringing people together in unity. The first word speaks of a bond of hope, confidence, trust and expectation. The second word speaks of firm belief, faith and certainty, especially when it comes to self-awareness and faith in ourselves.

Now let us look more closely at each of these words.

The first Sanskrit word is **ā-shā-bandha** (आशाबन्ध), a bond of hope, confidence, trust and expectation.

We experience the binding, uniting power of trust and confidence among colleagues, family and any group intent on a common enterprise.

The first two syllables "ā-shā" indicate a "wish, desire or hope."

"Bandha" is a bond or tie; a thing that unites.

This Sanskrit word "bandha" is the origin of English words like "bond, bound, and binding." We are concerned here with being bound to the positive, connected to the inspirational. We wish to be bound to our hopes and positive expectations. This frees us from division, from narrow bondage, and nurtures unity within ourselves.

Pāṇini helps us to understand this. He indicates that one of the places where a true bond is found is "in the act of connection." It is in leaving division and separation, and in finding unity and connection that we experience the meaning of "bandha."

So "ā-sha-bandha" means to unite and bind ourselves to our highest wish, hope and desire. When we do this, we change our reality. Instead of division, we see unity, instead of conflict we experience reconciliation. This naturally builds confidence to face a world that is welcoming and friendly.

The second Sanskrit word is **pratyaya** (प्रत्यय), meaning firm belief, faith, and certainty.

Pāṇini tells us that "studying and remembering" nurture firm belief, faith and certainty. The "study and memory" to which Pāṇini refers, is related to studying the words of the wise teachers who tell us how to achieve self-knowledge and self-awareness. Deep self-awareness inwardly unifies us by taking us beyond our inner divisions.

Our limited habitual thoughts and feelings, which divide us from ourselves and also from those around us, yield to deep self-awareness. When we become self-aware, we feel an alignment of body, mind, heart and spirit.

This inner unity, this non-division, gives us the strength and the freedom to move confidently in any direction.

Also, if we experience unity within ourselves, then we cannot help but see unity everywhere we look. Hermes Trismegistus, the sage of Ancient Egypt, tells us "as within so without."

So, to summarize, the Sanskrit indicators of Uniting speak of binding connections, firm belief, faith and self-awareness leading to inner unity. This inner unity naturally translates to the experience of unity in everything we meet. For example, if our mind, heart, spiritual beliefs and actions are aligned and united, then we have the strength, power and confidence to tackle challenges and opportunities as they arise.

We are like the brothers in the story. They started out competing with each other, then they discovered the strength and power of unity. They were joyful and were not only inwardly aligned but were also united as brothers.

Bringing Unity Out of Division

During my thirty years as a teacher of children, I met many students who demonstrated a fine ability to apply timeless wisdom. It showed in their deep connection with values and principles. I was touched by their sincerity. It showed that this wisdom is accessible to both young and old. Perhaps unbeknownst to them, their efforts always taught me a lot.

I particularly remember a group of twelve-year-old girls who were challenged to return to a feeling of unity and harmony.

During the lunchtime break the girls were in the playground enjoying a game and initially everything was harmonious. As the game progressed, a few things didn't go according to the rules. Some minor complaints built up and soon the "blame game" was in full swing. This led to personal criticisms and bad feelings. A situation that had been united, harmonious, and happy, had become divided and unhappy. No-one seemed able to budge from their fixed point of view.

A few of the girls in the group felt uncomfortable with this turn of events. They realized that arguing would not resolve the disagreements and reestablish unity and harmony; they needed to take another approach. They were prepared to work to restore everyone's enjoyment of the game and the unity of each other's company.

First, they suggested everyone take turns to say how they were feeling, and how they saw the situation. The girls agreed that only one person would speak at a time, and that the others would show respect and listen, even if they disagreed.

Because the girls listened to each other with full attention and respect, they all calmed down. They were able to agree on the common points in all their different accounts. Their focus shifted from the problem to the resolution of the disagreement. That is a skill in itself! Then they brainstormed a variety of solutions; all were fully engaged in reaching an agreement on the best way to move forward. This created a calm and intelligent space to resolve the disagreements. Sincere apologies were given and accepted on all sides. Happiness, harmony and unity were restored.

When the girls came back to class after playtime, they came up to me and said, "…we think we should report what has happened, just so you know." There certainly wasn't any bragging or wish for praise or reward. They were calm, respectful and matter-of-fact.

At this school, much class time and attention were given to the practical application of values and principles; not just learning the theory but actually how to apply these values in daily life, even if it's difficult. These girls were applying what they had learned. It is no mean feat to do this on your own at twelve years old, with friends in the heat of the moment.

Afterwards I reflected on what the girls had taught me.

These twelve-year-old girls valued the strength, power, and happiness of unity and harmony above division, unhappiness, and the desire to be "right." They were able to step over any personal ego and respect each other's viewpoints. Rather than staying trapped within the problem, they invested their valuable free playtime and were able to remain focused throughout and find a solution. It took more than just trying to be "nice" to each other; they had to work for it. They had to apply both love and reason. With the application of their intelligence, they found common ground. They brought unity out of division.

Practices

Key Embracing All Situations with Firm Self-Belief, Patience, and an Open Heart

Unity is completely natural. We have to work to create division. We become so accustomed to this constant effort of division, that we're unaware that it is fundamentally unnatural. If there is division within, we will create and experience division without—as within, so without—this is a law of the universe.

It takes quiet care and attention to become aware of any inner divisions, and then to release them to reveal unity. In truth, we don't create unity, we simply uncover it. Forcing the issue can create new divisions to replace old ones. While unity is natural, we might have to apply a little reason in order to find and experience it everywhere. Reason is that power of the mind which takes us beyond division and opens the door to unity. It does this by distinguishing truth from untruth, and reality from falsehood. The use of reason allows us to see beyond differences and connect with that unity which underlies appearances.

The following starter practice is a powerful exercise in the use of Reason to discover unity. In the process, we begin to see the world differently, changing from a world of division to a unified world of harmony.

Starter Finding the Unifying Factor, Looking Beyond Differences to Strengthen Reason

In this exercise we are going to use our power of reason to look beyond differences for the unifying factor. Some examples: we can look beyond apples and oranges and see fruit, or we can look beyond men and women and see human beings.

- Sit down with your journal or some paper and a pen. To begin with, take two things that have different characteristics, and look for the unifying factor, that shared principle or characteristic which both have.

- Write down ten examples with which you can connect and relate, e.g.:
    - Cat and Giraffe: the unifying factor is animal
    - Day and Night: the unifying factor is the Earth in relation to the Sun
    - Mother and Father: the unifying factor is child.

- Now take this practice another step when you're out during the day. As you go about your daily business find two things and discover the underlying factor that unites them both. For example, your desk and chair at work: the unifying factor is furniture. If any of these examples from your day stand out to you, make a note of them in your journal too.

- Now that you have practiced this exercise with two things, you can expand it out by increasing the number of elements you are seeking to unify. For example, a full train carriage is united by all the people being "commuters." You can take this even further by finding other commonalities that may not be so obvious, such as: they all needed to buy tickets, they all live in this city, they are all breathing air. Keep this enjoyable and light. It's fun to spot these hidden elements which unite every experience despite apparent differences. Write down examples that stand out.

Intermediate Expanding the Love, Letting Love Flow Freely

Find some time to sit quietly. Take a few deep breaths and become inwardly calm, still and present.

- Gently feel an expansion of your awareness. Remain at rest and bring to mind someone or something you love; this could be your spouse, partner, child, friend or pet.

- Feel love well-up and expand within you, and let it flow freely to the person or thing that you love.

- Now let this same love expand further, and flow to anyone or anything in the world that could do with some more love. Let the love expand like a wave or a sphere, growing as large as possible and including everything. Let this whole exercise be gentle and calm. Seek nothing in return for yourself.

- Repeat this practice with other positive emotions such as admiration or respect. For example, think of someone you admire and let that admiration expand. Remember to start from calm stillness and peace. Let the feeling expand and flow freely out. Hold nothing back and seek nothing for yourself in this practice. Don't look for any pay-off.

- If you feel peace, strength, fulfillment and contentment as a result of this practice, then send those feelings to whomever in the world needs a little more peace, strength, fulfillment and contentment.

- First practice this exercise on your own at home. Then extend out into your life when you're at work, out shopping or with family and friends.

Now how do you feel? Abundant, unified, present? Make any notes in your journal about the effect of this practice.

Advanced Letting Go of the Idea of "Other"

In this practice, you will let go of the idea of "other." This is a mysterious and powerful exercise where too much explanation will merely create more mental clutter. Sometimes we just have to embrace the mysterious.

- Set aside some time and sit quietly. Breathe deeply a few times and fall still with each breath. Become inwardly calm, still and present.

- Gently let your awareness expand. If you find the awareness stops, then simply let the awareness expand past that point. Don't force anything; let this be natural and easy.

- Allow the senses to receive sense impressions effortlessly.

- Allow the mind to let go of any idea of "other." Continue to rest in stillness and expanded awareness and gently keep letting go of any idea of "other." Spend three to five minutes, once a day for a week, doing this exercise.

This practice is quiet, calm and non-judgmental. Part of the mysterious aspect of this exercise is that everyone may have a different experience. Some may just experience a little peace, a little expansion of their being. Others may experience some form of energetic change, like a demarcation line between themselves and "other." There is no right and wrong experience from this practice.

Now that we have addressed the importance of Uniting and have tried some practical exercises to broaden our experience, we can move to the next part of F.U.S.E. Program. This is Simplifying, where we discover the power of staying with the essentials and letting go of the non-essentials.

Chapter Eleven

SIMPLIFYING

"Simplicity is the ultimate form of sophistication."

—Leonardo da Vinci

In this chapter we are going to look at Simplifying, the next element of the F.U.S.E. Program. "Simplifying" is the ability to stay with that which is essential and let go of the non-essentials such as past emotions, thoughts, and actions that aren't necessary anymore and complicate matters. This is how we maintain the characteristic energy of Simplifying which is straight, pure and true. The following story illustrates this.

Why Are You Still Carrying Her?

Two Zen monks were traveling together. They reached a river with a very strong current. As they made preparations to cross the river, they saw a beautiful young woman trying to cross as well. She politely asked the monks if they would help her cross the river. The two monks looked at each other for a moment. Being monks, they had taken a vow not to have any physical contact with women.

Then the older of the two monks stepped forward and gently picked up the young woman without saying a word. He carried her across the river and placed her carefully on the bank. The younger monk had followed behind, also in silence. The young woman thanked the older monk for his kind assistance and went on her way.

> The two monks continued on their journey; however, the younger monk was shocked at the actions of his companion. How could he do such a thing which is against their sacred vows?
>
> ◆
>
> They walked on for several hours without saying a word to each other. The younger monk's mind and heart was anything but peaceful; he was in turmoil about the events that had transpired at the river crossing. He was becoming exhausted and confused through merely thinking about this again and again.
>
> ◆
>
> Eventually he could stay silent no longer and he exclaimed to the older monk, "We are monks and we took a vow not to touch women in any way. How could you break the sacred vow and carry that woman across the river?"
>
> The older monk looked at his companion with a kind smile and said, "I put down the young woman on the other side of the river many hours ago. Why are you still carrying her?"

This story can reflect our experience. The two monks represent being able to let go of the past, and holding on to the past. The key lesson from the story is that the two monks symbolize either carrying thoughts, ideas, feelings and actions from the past that are no longer useful in the present, or Simplifying by putting them down.

There is a potent lesson in the action of carrying the beautiful young woman across the river, setting her down safely on the other side and then letting go of that event as the next part of the journey proceeds naturally and calmly.

The older monk in this simple Zen story teaches us about the power of Simplifying through letting go of what is unnecessary and living fully in the present. The younger monk illustrates our all too common experience of carrying around accumulations from the past such as anger, resentments and old hurts. We're left tired, lacking clarity and often unable to act freely and simply in the present.

For example, we may bring our old impressions of strict or tough teachers to every situation where we meet a teacher. This will obscure our view of whether this new teacher is different. We do the same in other situations as well.

We can choose to let go of that which is not essential; which doesn't serve us anymore. With simplicity comes peace, lightness and clarity. This creates the mental and emotional space to be able to respond fully and appropriately to the next opportunity that life sends us. These are essential qualities in Conscious Confidence.

What Does Sanskrit Teach Us about Simplifying?

The essence of simplicity is letting go of unnecessary things in our lives. This can be physical in the form of hoarded possessions, mental in the form of limiting beliefs, or emotional like resentments or long past hurts. We can even let go of unhelpful attitudes like sloth and delay. Letting go leads to Simplifying, which makes it easier to see clearly, be strong and confident, and move forward unimpeded.

The essential energy of Simplifying is to be straight, pure and true. Three Sanskrit words meaning "confidence" relate to Simplifying: the first means uncluttered, not accumulating excess in body, mind and heart. The second word means clear and certain, and the third word means free of weakness, sloth and doubt.

Now let's look into the deeper meanings of these three words.

A-san-deha (अमन्देह) uncluttered, not accumulating excess in body, mind and heart which results in a lack of confusion.

A-san-digdha (अमन्दिग्ध) clear, certain, distinct.

A-sam-shaya (अमंशय) absence of feebleness and sloth, absence of doubt, awake and resolute.

A characteristic energy of these words is Simplifying, because they all require a "letting go" of the non-essential. The first thing to notice in the three words "a-san-deha," "a-san-digdha" and "a-sam-shaya," is that they all have one tiny but important sound "a" at the beginning. When placed at the beginning of words "a" means "not."

"A-san-deha" and "a-san-digdha" are similar in that they both speak of not accumulating excess, not being covered over, not being confused and perplexed. "A-saṃ-shaya," means not weak, feeble, slothful and full of doubt.

Imagine a hoarder's house that is full of clutter. Every room, corridor, nook and cranny filled with piles of things that once had a purpose but are now no longer needed. Add to that the buildup of grime and dust on the windows and surfaces.

The owners of the house are weighed down by accumulations from the past in the form of possessions and dirt. They are unclear, they don't know what to do. They are holding onto the past.

Now they want to sell the house.

A real estate agent tells them that in order to sell the property, they have to de-clutter and let go of the excess accumulation. This is "a-san-deha." When the house is free of excess belongings, the accumulated grime and dirt has to be cleaned off the windows, walls and floors. This is "a-san-digdha." Both are necessary for the situation to move forward, for the owners to be free.

Before the clean-up, the owners lacked the clarity and energy to act. They needed certainty and resolve leading to purposeful effective action to get the house ready for sale. This energy and resolve associated with being able to simplify is "a-saṃ-shaya."

The essence of Simplifying is letting go. What are we letting go? We let go of that which is unhelpful, limiting and negative in our lives. This uncovers a new energy, a new approach to life which is straight, true and pure, in the sense of being uncluttered by distracting irrelevancies.

> "Our life is frittered away by detail. Simplify, simplify, simplify!"
>
> —Henry David Thoreau

Just Another Activity

It was summer time in Australia during the annual vacation period. A father, mother and fourteen-year-old daughter were holidaying with their extended family. All the generations were there: parents, grandparents, aunts and uncles, siblings and cousins.

The parents of this fourteen-year-old girl were keen seekers of wisdom, and practiced meditation twice a day for half an hour. They were conscientious to find somewhere quiet and appropriate to do this. Their daughter had grown up with this example from her parents. When she was old enough, she wanted to meditate as well. She started with ten minutes twice a day. She found this was easy and natural, ten minutes before school and ten minutes in the evening.

One evening during this family vacation, it was nearing dinner time. Some adults were in the kitchen cooking and chatting. The children, all siblings and cousins, including the girl, were sitting around on the floor playing board games and cards. The remaining adults were watching the evening news on television. There was also some music playing in the background.

The parents of this girl, having gone somewhere quiet to meditate, returned to the lounge room and asked their daughter if she had meditated yet. There was still time to do it before dinner.

She had been so engaged in playing with her cousins that she had completely forgotten and had lost track of the time.

Her approach was simple. She just excused herself from the game, got up from the floor and sat on the couch, closed her eyes and began to meditate there and then. She saw no difference between her meditating, and everyone else doing what they were doing. It was just one other activity in the room. She was open and confident, not embarrassed or shy. The adults were still cooking, the television was still on, the music was still playing, and the other children continued their games.

After a few moments, everyone became aware that she was meditating and the other children naturally started speaking softly and quietly, the adults in the kitchen stopped chatting loudly and quieted the sounds of pots and pans as they cooked, and someone turned the volume down on the music and the television. It wasn't because she required anyone else to change what they were doing. They simply did it out of respect, to support her.

Her parents, who had expected her to go away to a quiet place, were surprised that she didn't. They watched the whole scene change. She didn't need to go to a quiet place, she brought quiet to the place where she was. Everyone quite naturally encompassed this girl meditating and enjoyed the quiet calm and space that it provided after a busy day.

At the conclusion of her ten minutes of meditation, the family hustle and bustle continued as they all sat down to enjoy dinner together.

Practices

Key Staying with the Essentials, Letting Go of the Non-Essentials

Sanskrit is quite clear about confidence, certainty and trust arising from an absence of clutter and confusion.

Let's start with the physical. Physical clutter can reflect our mental and emotional state. "As within so without," the outer reflects the inner world. Commit to this Physical Clean–Up exercise and note the energy and clarity released in the mental and emotional areas. See how this small start can expand into other contexts in your life.

Starter The Physical Clean-Up

Choose a drawer, a shelf, your desk or your room. Tidy it up, de-clutter and clean it from top to bottom.

- De-clutter: You should aim to give away, recycle, or throw out at least three items you no longer use.

- Create Order: Put things in their place, and if they don't have a place then find one. Create some order with your belongings.

- Clean Up: Start cleaning from the top to the bottom. Get into the corners and high shelves and areas out of sight. Move the furniture and clean underneath it.

- Create Beauty: Put all the furniture back with care. Consider its arrangement so the room is practical and pleasant.

Intermediate The Mental Clean-Up

Now it is time to simplify the mental level. Preparation: Sit down outside or in a freshly cleaned area with a pen and your journal, a note book or some paper. Take a few moments to relax and breathe deeply. Feel a sense of calm and expansion.

- Step One: Consider your talents and strengths. What are you good at? Where do you shine? What comes easily? What do you apply yourself to? What do others say about you? What activities make you happy? Write the answers down.

- Step Two: Reflect on any ideas you have about yourself and your situation that seem to get in the way of giving full expression and commitment to the above talents, qualities and strengths. For example: I'm not good enough, I'll fail, I don't have the qualifications or experience, I don't have the money, I'll never get my family to go along with my plan.

- Step Three: Take a few deep breaths and return to inner peace.

- Step Four: Once you're still, examine these limiting ideas from that place of peace and simply ask yourself questions such as: Are these ideas true? Do they need to hold me back? Can I find a way through? What is a way around any of these limitations? Am I ready and willing to let go of these limitations and confidently take the next step to give full expression to the best of myself? If I had all the time in the world what could I do? If I knew I could not fail what could I do?

- Step Five: Now write down three action steps you could take straight away to start moving towards expressing your talents, strengths and qualities from Step One.

- Step Six: Now actually take the first step. Take resolute and purposeful action.

Advanced The Emotional Clean-Up

Preparation: Sit quietly in a fresh and clean area, or outside. Have a pen and your journal or some paper with you. Now take a few deep breaths and relax. Let go and feel a sense of calm and stillness. Allow your awareness to open up and expand.

- Step One: Write down the name of someone—a co-worker, your boss, a neighbor—who prompts the rise of negative feelings.

- Step Two: In a few words write down your feelings. Keep it simple.

- Step Three: Now think of your nominated person again, consider them afresh, imagine meeting them for the first time. Note something positive, something real. It could be their smile, their generosity, their skill. Remember this is for the first time. There is no past history. Have some fun with this, after all what have you got to lose?

- Step Four: Write down these positive feelings about this person.

- Step Five: Next time you see this person try meeting them as if for the first time and remember something positive.

Now that we have looked at the importance of Simplifying, and have tried some practical exercises to declutter and clear the way, we move to the final part of F.U.S.E. Program. This is Energizing, where we live each day with enthusiasm, creativity and vitality.

Chapter Twelve

Energizing

"Our doubts are traitors and make us lose the good
we oft might win, by fearing to attempt."

—William Shakespeare,
Measure for Measure (Act 1, Scene 4)

In this chapter we are going to look at Energizing, the final element of the F.U.S.E. Program. "Energizing" has the characteristic energy of being dynamic, creative and enthusiastic. All the exercises in the previous chapter on "Simplifying" are designed to de-clutter, clarify and make us resolute in order to prepare us to live each day with enthusiasm, creativity and vitality.

The following story shows how a narrow and uncreative approach to problem solving consumes energy and results in unhappiness and dissatisfaction. The story also shows the liberating, fulfilling and Energizing effect of taking creative and unselfish action.

A Story of Heaven and Hell

Once a man was being instructed by his spiritual teacher and mentor about heaven and hell.

"Heaven and hell are here right now in front of us," the teacher said calmly.

"What do you mean? How can this be?" the student queried, his brow furrowed. "Don't we go to either heaven or hell after death depending on our actions during life?"

♦

"There's no waiting that long, you get to choose where you want to live every moment of the day. It's a simple menu of two choices, either heaven or hell," the teacher replied with a gentle smile.

"Can you please explain further?" the student persisted.

◆

"Imagine there are two identical magnificent banquets. Both the banquet halls are gloriously decorated. There is such beauty to behold everywhere the eye falls, and awe-inspiring detailed care in how it's all arranged. The banquet tables are overflowing with every possible food and delicacy.

Remember that both banquets are identical down to every precise detail.

Seated around the vast tables in both banquet halls are identical guests. The same people are at each banquet simultaneously.

◆

The one unusual feature of both the banquets is that the guests have been given spoons with very long handles. The spoon handles are five feet long, and they can only eat the food with this cutlery.

In one of the banquet halls, the guests are very unhappy. They are starving. Some just sit motionless staring at the food, while others whine and complain at how they can't reach the food and how it's so unfair. They feel sorry for themselves. There are other guests who repeatedly try to pick up the food with their five-foot spoons. They stretch and contort their bodies to get the food into their mouths with the long handles, but the food spills everywhere. Of course, they can't reach their mouths, so they become increasingly angry and frustrated. They shout, criticize and blame everyone else. They feel like victims, powerless to free themselves from the situation.

The whole scene is awful to watch and even worse to experience for the people.

◆

Contrast that with the other identical banquet hall. This is quite different. They have the exact same five-foot-long spoons, yet everyone is happily enjoying all the abundant, delicious food. There's absolutely no problem eating it. The guests are all chatting enthusiastically, there's laughter, merriment and good company. All the guests are fully satisfied on every level."

♦

The teacher paused to see if his student was following this extraordinary scene thus far.

"How did the guests who were having such a wonderful time achieve this?" the student asked in amazement.

"The solution was very simple," the teacher continued. "The guests who were happily eating, enjoying themselves and fully satisfied, were picking up the food with their long-handled spoons and feeding each other. They could see that the problem lay in trying to feed only themselves regardless of anyone else.

"They had great fun selecting food for a different person and then feeding it to them. This also happened in return. No one went without. Everyone was completely focused on serving each other so that everyone was fully satisfied."

♦

The student was perplexed, "What of the guests in the other banquet hall? Why didn't they do this too? It seems so obvious!"

The teacher chuckled quietly, "This is a question of levels of consciousness, awareness and energy. At a higher level of awareness and consciousness, solutions like this are simple and obvious. Energy is available to take ownership and act productively. However, at a lower level of consciousness with a more limited awareness, these choices didn't occur to the unhappy diners. No one thought of how they could solve the problem. It's the same as being asleep in bed at night when you're unaware of anything."

♦

The teacher went on to explain, "This is how heaven and hell are here right now and it's your choice where you want to abide.

The same abundant life is available to everyone. It takes greater awareness and higher levels of consciousness to realize this.

"Heaven is where we partake of the joy, abundance and magnificence through taking intelligent action in service of all. This is how everyone is satisfied and fulfilled. You have an abundance of energy because you are not wasting it being angry, bitter and resentful, and trying to take care of yourself alone.

"Hell is where we exist in the same wonderful abundance, but we miss out on it because our energy is wasted in negativity and in thinking only about how we will cater for ourselves with no thought for anyone else. This leads to misery, aloneness, and lack. We feel sorry for ourselves and blame others and the situation. The more we try to look after ourselves without any regard for others, we become increasingly frustrated and angry.

"It is a choice that only an individual can make. Both are spread before us all the time."

~ this story appears in many traditions such as Confucian, Hindu and Jewish

This story has a powerful and clear message. In Hell, the world of selfish action, the diners lacked the energy to find a solution to their problem. They were mired in a world of blame and resentment, and exhausted by trying to solve their problems on their own. In Heaven the diners, who thought of service to others, were energized, creative and happy.

Life is a wonderful banquet of possibilities. Fulfillment and happiness are the natural outcome if we approach life with open-hearted enthusiasm, creativity, and energy. The way to do this is to develop our talents, strengths and qualities, and then to use them to benefit not only ourselves but others too. For example, a doctor studies for years and uses their talents to cure people. An entrepreneur invests their time and money to turn an idea into a business. They provide a service or product about which they are passionate, and which solves a problem or meets a need in the market place. In this way, everyone benefits.

What Does Sanskrit Teach Us about Energizing?

Two Sanskrit words for confidence are "vi-shvāsa" and "sam-ā-shvāsa." These two words center on breath and breathing, which are the basis of life and energy. The first word "vi-shvāsa" means freedom from fear, and the second word "sam-ā-shvāsa" means to take courage. Let's explore each of these two Sanskrit words and their deeper meanings.

Vi-shvāsa (विश्वास) to breathe freely and be free from fear and apprehension; to be full of trust and confidence.

Sam-ā-shvāsa (समाश्वास) to breathe again; to revive; take courage. These two words have the same central element—shvāsa—which means: To breathe, respire, draw breath. Breath and breathing are fundamental to life.

Pāṇini tells us that the meaning of "shvāsa" will be found in "prāṇa." In Sanskrit, "prāṇa" (प्राण) is the word for the "life force." If you have learnt some yoga, you will have come across this word "prāṇa." It means "the breath of life, spirit and vitality."

Spirit, life and breath are intimately connected. *The Bhagavad Gītā* teaches that everyone is linked by the breath as "pearls strung on a thread." All our lives, all the individuals walking around in separate bodies partaking of this life force, are strung together on the breath of life, like pearls strung together on a silken thread.

Notice how we use this life force via the act of breathing to change our energetic state. When we're fearful we take a deep breath to calm down and steady ourselves. When we're slothful and we want to become energized, we take a deep breath first and then get moving. When we feel a bit down and want to pick ourselves up, we take a deep breath and then choose a positive attitude and cheer up.

This animating, energizing breath gives confidence. It frees us from fear and leads to creative dynamic action. We take heart because there is no place here for feebleness, insecurity and inertia.

If you desire certainty, clarity and success then now is the time to practice Energizing, to take purposeful transformative action. The characteristic energy in this final part of the F.U.S.E. Program is dynamic, creative and enthusiastic.

The Campsite Trek

A young woman, let's call her Donna, was in her last year of high school and participating in an extra-curricular outdoor wilderness survival program especially designed for young people growing up in big cities. Donna and her friends taking the program had known and trusted each other since the early days of elementary school. All the students had to take a series of long treks and several overnight camping trips in remote areas.

The level of difficulty of the final outdoor trip was high. It was a five-day trek and the area was remote and rugged, and there were steep climbs. The students were required to carry their own provisions and equipment. They were trained in practical skills such as map reading, outdoor cooking and first-aid. The training also included personal and inter-personal development with team building, resilience and leadership activities.

The long treks and overnight camps were intended to challenge the students to apply their training and adapt to real-life conditions.

It was day three and the weather had turned cold and wet. The group had walked all day and they were tired. They had started out positive and had been encouraging each other. However, in the final hours before reaching their overnight camp location, Donna noticed how the conversation changed amongst the group.

There were complaints of sore feet and aching muscles, and how tired, cold and wet they were.

Then the talk became critical of each other; jibes at how annoying they found some behaviors. They even started rehashing things from childhood.

Donna resolved not to judge her friends. She listened to it all but didn't join in. She encouraged everyone to keep going despite the arguing. Donna knew that they needed to focus their energy.

Upon successfully reaching their place to make camp for the night, her friends simply sat down and continued to complain.

Donna, on the other hand, gathered sticks and logs, and lit a fire. Her friends sat down to warm themselves. Donna erected the tent. Once inside the comfort of the tent, her friends changed into dry clothes and began to calm down. Donna proceeded to prepare some hot food. Some of her friends were, by now, motivated to assist.

After the meal and some time in front of the fire, they were able to reflect and learn from what had happened. They appreciated Donna's focused action, resilience and patient care for them all in the face of challenging circumstances. They could see how their emotional childish squabbling wasn't a good use of their energy reserves.

Donna's practical leadership and effective action demonstrated her discipline, inner strength and care. She resolved not to judge her friends or to take on a role of being a martyr. She understood what was happening and simply set about doing what was needed.

This scenario is a good example of the power of the four-fold energy of Conscious Confidence in practice. Donna was focused and strong throughout. Her compassion and understanding restored unity within the group. Donna let go of any resentments and judgments and simplified the situation by doing only what was needed. At each point she was energized and took dynamic and effective action.

Practices

Key Living Each Day with Enthusiasm, Creativity, and Vitality

Starter The Power of Completing Unfinished Tasks

Consider all the partially completed tasks you have at home and at work. You know the sort of things: the dishes that haven't been washed, your bed hasn't been made, the overflowing in-tray at work. We don't complete tasks because we are distracted, or we simply run out of energy. So we live with dirty dishes, unmade beds and laundry baskets full of unfolded clothes sitting around until we can get to them.

- Pick one or two easy tasks that you haven't completed today or this week. Nothing major; simple things such as folding all your clean laundry, making your bed or tidying your desk.

- Note any feelings that may arise at the prospect of completing these tasks. It could be a sense of mild anxiety that you have many, far more important, things to do than this. Perhaps the feelings could be irritation and annoyance, or even a general sense of heaviness, boredom, and what could be described as "Blah!" Be awake and aware of these feelings. They are not real, they are just passing movements of energy. You are far greater than any of these limiting feelings.

- Act despite them. Act because the task is there to be done. The purpose is to allow that activity to be completed so it can come to rest. Otherwise the energy of the task is left hanging and unresolved.

- Note how you feel once these tasks are actually complete. Stick at this practice for a week and note the difference. Deliberately complete one or two simple tasks every day. Once the momentum is up, you may find yourself extending this to more tasks.

Intermediate Honoring the Gift of Speech

This exercise is about stopping our negative and useless speech, even when it is inner self-talk. Mindless, idle, useless or negative and destructive speech are habits that, unless consciously restrained, can govern whole areas of our life. If we had some understanding of how our world is created by our speech, we would stop useless and negative talk immediately.

- Useless speech takes different forms, such as speaking when no one is listening, or continuing to speak when other people are sending you signs that they are tired of listening. Another example is over-explaining something or being long-winded in telling a story. Idle repetition, or speaking as if you know about something when you don't, are other types of useless speech.
  Negative speech can range from being petty and nit-picking through to cruel and destructive. For example: finding fault, unkind criticism, intimidating others, or drowning out other people's opinions.

- To deal with these forms of speech, first you must become aware of them. Any negative or useless speech should be noted. Simply become aware of it. Don't judge, just observe.

- Once you have identified the speech, the next step is to stop it. Keep up normal conversation and other interactions but restrain your habit of useless or negative speech.

- Sometimes it's best just to stop speaking until you have something more uplifting to say. Praise is always good! Find something positive to speak about or ask an intelligent question about something the other person is interested in.

If, as a result of this practice, you find that you don't have much to say, then this is useful information.

Advanced The Power of Helping Others

This is doing something for someone else. The task can be simple. The key elements of this exercise are:

- That the task needs to be done.

- That it is performed with your own hands (so no getting your kids to do it for you, or paying someone to do it!).

- That you don't make a big deal that you've done it.

- That your main motivation is not the reward, credit, acknowledgement or appreciation for doing the task.

For example, taking a few minutes to wash up the cups left in the sink at work, hanging up your partner's towel in the bathroom. If you are unsure what to do, then spend a little time at home and see if there is something you could do for your spouse or partner, or you could see if there is something at work for a co-worker.

A word of caution: Sometimes the real service is to get your teenager to pick up their own socks, or your colleagues to wash up their own cups.

This practice is meant to be simply lending a hand to others with no benefit to yourself other than perhaps a thank you and sometimes not even that. Have fun and be a bit creative with this practice. You could look for things to do that you don't ordinarily notice.

If you are one of those people who are always picking up after others for example, and perhaps feel like a martyr or experience some resentment for being exploited, then you might like to do this practice by finding a harmonious way to encourage others to fulfil their responsibilities.

This practice of service, in whatever form it takes, is energizing. That energy will be available for taking further dynamic, creative and enthusiastic action.

Now that we have looked at Energizing, the final element of the six parts of the F.U.S.E. Program, we will bring it all together in the next chapter by setting out the entire program from Core Values onwards. We will also give some guidance about effective implementation of the F.U.S.E. Program including: practicing regardless of distractions and demands of daily life, having the courage to take the next step even if it is into the dark, and lastly, the power of goal-setting to achieve success.

Chapter Thirteen

LIGHT THE F.U.S.E. TO MAKE CONSCIOUS CONFIDENCE A REALITY

> "If we are peaceful, if we are happy, we can smile,
> and everyone in our family, our entire society,
> will benefit from our peace."
>
> —Thich Nhat Hanh, Vietnamese Buddhist Monk

The aim of this chapter is to make Conscious Confidence a reality in your life. The message of the following story of Narada and the Jar of Oil is that any effort that we make is valuable in applying the F.U.S.E. Program that is set out after the story.

Narada and the Jar of Oil

There was a holy sage called Narada who dwelt blissfully in the divine realm. He spent all his time playing his musical instrument and singing songs and prayers of devotion to his beloved guru Lord Vishnu.

One day a thought appeared in Narada's mind, "I spend every day singing and praying to my divine guru. Surely I am Lord Vishnu's greatest devotee." This thought stayed with him, and he felt rather proud of his devotion, faith and commitment.

A few days later he decided that he wanted to hear this from his Lord's lips, so he went to see Lord Vishnu.

♦

With hands clasped in devotion and bowing low, he respectfully asked, "My Lord, am I your greatest devotee?"

Lord Vishnu smiled gently and said, "Yes, dear Narada, you are certainly one of my greatest devotees, but there is another who is greater even than you."

Narada was shocked, this was not the reply he was expecting.

"Who is this great devotee of yours?" said Narada, "I should like to meet him. Where does he dwell? What has he done to earn this title?"

"If you wish," Lord Vishnu replied, "we can visit him together."

Narada eagerly agreed.

◆

So, through Vishnu's divine powers, they found themselves on earth disguised as ordinary travelers; their divine forms concealed. They were standing before a humble farmhouse.

"This is where my greatest devotee lives with his family," said Lord Vishnu.

Vishnu knocked on the door, and a young girl opened it.

"Greetings," she said bowing to the unexpected visitors.

Lord Vishnu and Narada returned the greeting.

"Who's there?" called her father, who was the farmer who owned the house and the surrounding fields.

"Guests," said the girl, "two travelers."

"Invite them in at once," called her father, "they must join us for dinner."

◆

The girl ushered the disguised Vishnu and Narada into the house and they were warmly greeted by the farmer, his wife and all the family. Little did they know who their guests really were!

Vishnu and Narada washed their hands and sat with the family around the dinner table. The farmer said a few short prayers of devotion before everyone enjoyed the simple meal. After dinner, Narada and Vishnu were given a bed for the night.

◆

In the morning, the farmer recited some more prayers before breakfast, and invited his guests to join him as he went about his work on the farm that day.

Throughout the day, Vishnu and Narada watched the farmer attend to his work. He had much to do, but he often took the time to stop and offer a short prayer to the lord. The prayer was simple, but his intent was sincere. He also hummed hymns of praise as he worked.

He had no idea that his guests, the travelers, were actually his beloved Lord Vishnu and divine Narada.

At the end of the day, Vishnu and Narada gave thanks to the farmer and his family for their hospitality and left.

They walked away down the road in silence. After a short distance, Narada could contain himself no longer.

◆

"My lord," he asked, "I am perplexed. How is it possible that this farmer is your greatest devotee? He is devoted to you to be sure, but he works on his farm all day, and only says short simple prayers at certain times of the day. I sing songs of praise to you all day. Surely my intense devotion is greater than his?"

Lord Vishnu stopped and looked thoughtful, then he said, "Perhaps, Narada, you are right. Perhaps you are my greatest devotee. Will you do something for me?"

Narada was overjoyed!

"Yes, Lord, anything," he cried.

◆

Vishnu said, "Go and fetch an empty jar and a bottle of oil."

Narada, promptly fulfilled this request.

"Fill the jar with the oil," said Vishnu.

Narada eagerly filled the jar to the brim with the oil.

"Now Narada," said the Lord, "place the jar of oil on your head and walk around this small hill without spilling a drop. I will be waiting for you when you return."

◆

Narada, ever keen to prove himself the greatest of devotees, set himself to this odd task. He walked step by step around the hill taking great care not to spill a drop.

Finally, he returned. He carefully set the jar down at Lord Vishnu's feet.

"There," he cried, "I didn't spill a drop, just as you instructed!"

"Wonderful, Narada!" Lord Vishnu exclaimed. "You are truly a great devotee. However, may I ask how many times you thought of me as you walked around the hill? How many songs of devotion did you sing? How many prayers did you recite to me?"

"None," Narada stammered, "I was too busy concentrating on the jar of oil."

♦

Vishnu, with a kind smile, explained to Narada, "The effort not to spill one drop of oil, drove all thoughts of me from your mind. The farmer has much more to think about than one jar of oil. He has a wife, children, animals, crops and fields to care for every day. Yet, throughout the day doing all his work and attending to his responsibilities, he is still able to remember me with prayers, songs and devotions. Tell me Narada, who do you think is the greater devotee?"

Narada humbly bowed to Lord Vishnu and praised the farmer as the greater devotee.

This story illustrates the power of practice in daily life. In the farmer's case it involved prayers to Vishnu. In our life it can mean giving time and energy to any of the practices in this book despite distractions and other calls on our time and energy.

What Does Sanskrit Tell Us about Proceeding to Our Goal?

There is a traditional Sanskrit saying which contains an especially relevant philosophical meaning for us now: **padam padam prati padam arhati iti prātipadikam** पदम् पदम् प्रति पदम् । अर्हति इति प्रातिपदिकम् ॥ This saying means "Step by step, at every step awaits what is needed for that step."

Whenever we take a step, we discover whatever we need to know. Sometimes moving forward requires courage, because often, until we take a step in life, we actually don't know what we will find. This is essential advice as we embark on the F.U.S.E. Program. It is important to keep moving forward even when it is not clear what the next step will bring. You have now learned the six elements of the F.U.S.E. Program:

- Core Values
- Positive Attitude
- Focusing
- Uniting
- Simplifying
- Energizing

Each has been covered in a previous chapter, and at the end of each chapter there are specific practices designed to give you an experience of that level. Below is a summary of each level.

The F.U.S.E. Program

The F.U.S.E. Program is a series of practical step-by-step exercises drawn from timeless wisdom that lead you to Conscious Confidence.

It starts with the discovery and examination of our Core Values which we hold dear in our hearts. These values such as honesty, kindness, courage, freedom, or a combination of several, form a foundation from which we can move to the second element, a Positive Attitude.

With this positive outlook we experience an expansive, optimistic and creative approach to everything we meet.

The next phase is the four-fold energies: Focusing, Uniting, Simplifying, and Energizing. These four are derived from several Sanskrit words that mean "confidence." The F.U.S.E. Program, applied in this order, from the discovery of Core Values through to Energizing, allows us to make Conscious Confidence a reality.

You will find the recommended practices for each phase listed as key, starter, intermediate and advanced practices:

K = Key Practice   S = Starter Practice
I = Intermediate Practice   A = Advanced Practice

Core Values

The foundation of Conscious Confidence starts by connecting with your Core Values, who you really are, that which is most important to you. This is the heart of your true being. The story of the Values on the holiday island, tells us that we need a balance of Values and that Love is the key. The story of the five princes shows us that our Core Values are innate, they are an essential part of who we are.

The characteristic energy of Core Values is: Stillness, peace and inner self-knowledge.

The Sanskrit meaning for Core Values is: Your system of self-belief, the values that are the root or foundation of who you are, and the qualities or virtues that you honor and respect above all others.

Practices
K   Being Self-Aware and Self-Connected
S   Exploring Values
I   Discovering Your Own Core Values
A   Taking Your Core Values into Action

Positive Attitude

Your attitude is made up of your point of view, your intent, and your conduct. What you experience is affected by your attitude. With a Positive Attitude, we focus on solutions rather than problems, which leaves us energized, optimistic and motivated. We see opportunities which is an essential key to success. We see the white paper not the black dot, we aim for success, and like the frog in the race, block our ears to the voices that tell us we can't succeed.

The characteristic energy of a Positive Attitude is: Open, generous, full of potential and motivated.

The Sanskrit meaning for Positive Attitude is: Positive viewpoint, generous intent and right conduct.

Practices

K Choosing Openness, Optimism, and Strength in Your Approach to the World and Yourself

S Count Your Blessings: An exercise in gratitude.

I Start the Day Right! Upon waking, decide that you will have a positive attitude today no matter what.

A The Whole World is Your Teacher. We can learn something valuable from everyone we meet and everything that happens to us.

Focusing

Focusing is the power to give our attention fully where it is needed, rather than have it stolen away by distractions. Be focused on the eye of the bird in the tree and nothing else, just like Arjuna when he aimed his arrow.

The characteristic energy of Focusing is: Decisive, courageous and steady.

The Sanskrit meaning for Focusing: Focusing is derived from three Sanskrit words for confidence that stand for: firm belief, calm faith and conviction.

Practices

K Giving Undistracted Attention

S One Task Magic: Give full attention to one simple task every day.

I Self-Investment.
Reflection: Each day invest in your inner growth and inner prosperity.
The Witness: Spend a few minutes each day being still and aware.

A Seeking Higher Knowledge. When you don't know what to do, ask yourself: "What would a wise man or woman do here?"

Uniting

Uniting is the power that binds us all together, building trust and confidence. It is recognizing commonalities among things that seem on the surface to be different. Inner unity comes from faith and belief in ourselves. Be like the sons in the story who discovered the strength of unity in a bundle of sticks.

The characteristic energy of Uniting is: Compassionate, loving and supportive.

The Sanskrit meaning for Uniting: Uniting is derived from two Sanskrit words for confidence that mean binding connections, faith and firm self-belief leading to inner unity.

Practices

K Embracing All Situations with Firm Self-Belief, Patience, and an Open Heart

S Finding the Unifying Factor, Looking Beyond Differences to Strengthen Reason

I Expanding the Love, Letting Love Flow Freely

A Letting Go of the Idea of "Other"

Simplifying

Simplifying is staying with what is essential and letting go of what is non-essential. Like the monk carrying the woman across the river, let go of past feelings, thoughts, and actions that are no longer needed.

The characteristic energy of Simplifying is: Straight, true and pure.
The Sanskrit meaning for Simplifying: Simplifying is derived from three Sanskrit words for confidence that mean: uncluttered, clear and certain, awake and resolute.

Practices

K Staying with the Essentials and Letting Go of the Non-Essentials

S The Physical Clean-Up

I The Mental Clean-Up. Identifying and letting go of ideas that limit our ability to give full expression to our talents and strengths.

A The Emotional Clean-Up. Thinking about someone who triggers negative feelings and meeting them positively, as if for the first time.

Energizing

Energizing is living a courageous life that is creative, joyful and open-hearted, just like the diners in the story who fed each other and lived in Heaven. We remain vigilant to avoid the things in our lives that consume energy like negative self-talk and uncompleted tasks, and unnecessary distractions.

The characteristic energy of Energizing is: Dynamic, creative and enthusiastic.

The Sanskrit meaning for Energizing: Energizing is derived from two Sanskrit words for confidence that mean: freedom from fear, and to take courage.

Practices

- K Living Each Day with Enthusiasm, Creativity, and Vitality
- S The Power of Completing Unfinished Tasks
- I Honoring the Gift of Speech. Stopping our negative and useless speech, even when it is inner self-talk.
- A The Power of Helping Others

Implementing the F.U.S.E. Program

Now that we have laid out the F.U.S.E. Program the question is how to go about implementing the knowledge set out in this book.

First, read as much of the explanatory text in each chapter as you find useful. Perhaps you especially enjoyed the stories or maybe the Sanskrit meanings resonated with you the most. Then get started on the practices that are at the end of each chapter. Do the ones that appeal to you, as often and for as long as you can. Your authentic experience of the effect of these practices is where real transformation of information into wisdom occurs.

Some people experience an initial "high," sometimes followed by a dip. It is good to know this in advance so you can keep at the practices during those times. In my extensive experience of this kind of endeavor, I know that something very important is happening at a deeper level. Once again, keep practicing.

The following story illustrates the process of taking one step at a time. It is a journey that moves from one pool of light to the next.

A Series of Lamp Posts

A woman was inspired to change her career. She wanted to leave her corporate job. She wanted to become a mentor, a coach and support people. She felt that she had something unique to offer. She could sense that she had a life purpose, and it was calling to her from within her heart. Something had awoken within her, and it wasn't going back to sleep!

For quite a while, she had been feeling stuck and unfulfilled in her corporate role, but out of fear she stayed in her familiar environment. She felt confident, efficient and competent within that comfort zone.

Now, with the desire to move into the unknown, she was plagued by a lack of self-confidence, and this was unfamiliar. She didn't think she had the ability, she felt unqualified, and she couldn't believe that anyone would take her seriously. There was no rule book about how she was going to establish herself in this new role. There just seemed to be so much to do and she didn't know what her first step would be.

Making the move was scary. How would she start? What would she do? Who could she ask? She was both excited and terrified.

She sought advice, and one of her mentors told her the analogy of lamp posts set at intervals along a dark road. While the end of the road is in darkness, the journey can be taken safely by traveling from the light of one lamp post to the next.

She realized all she needed to do was take the first step, and then another step, and another. She knew there would be the right knowledge, energy and motivation to take each step.

With patience, steadiness and a positive attitude, she had faith she would reach her destination and achieve her goal. There would always be another lamp post lighting the next part of her road, so she didn't have to worry about knowing every step ahead of time.

This form of "padam, padam"—step by step—was what she needed to learn. This showed her what she needed to do. She needed to have faith and trust in herself, and in the abundance of the present moment. There would always be the right knowledge, energy and intelligence required for each step. This was a new and different way of living, and it felt right.

So, she started by steadily and courageously taking one step at a time.

She kept her focus on the one thing she was doing. This took practice, because there were often distracting thoughts about what she had to do next, and whether she would be a success. However, she resolved to proceed step by step.

With patience, perseverance and consistently choosing to be positive and of good cheer, she has created a new life for herself doing what she loves. She feels she is giving the very best of what she has to offer, and her clients agree that she has helped them transform their lives too.

The Power of Goal-Setting

Actual practice is the key to harnessing the timeless wisdom of Sanskrit. This commitment to making it part of your life will lead to certainty, clarity and success. Start with one or two practices from this book that call out to you; practices that you feel drawn to.

One technique for making practice more effective and successful is to link it with goal-setting. Set a realistic goal for practicing. Decide what you want and clarify it by checking if it is S.M.A.R.T.:

Specific and significant
Measurable and meaningful
Achievable and action-oriented
Realistic and rewarding
Time-bound and trackable

For example: The Physical Clean Up (the Starter Practice in "Simplifying").

Specific and significant: "I set a goal to address the mess in the top drawer of my bedroom dresser; it contains things of value to me and it's always a mess, and I never get around to cleaning it up."

Measurable and meaningful: "This task has a clear beginning and end; it will make it easier to find things and I would like my valuables to be in order. I will clean the top drawer and not all the drawers. The top drawer matters the most to me because it is the messiest place in my house. I can never find anything there without a lot of looking, so this goal of cleaning the top dresser drawer is meaningful for me."

Achievable and action-oriented: "I am able to complete this task; it is a task to do and not something to think about. It is not a huge task."

Should the task you identify at first feel too big, start with a small portion of it. Cleaning up the dresser drawer might be the beginning to cleaning up your entire bedroom, which might feel overwhelming and unachievable as a first task.

Realistic and rewarding: "Cleaning up my top drawer is realistic; it is my space and I can choose to clean it and keep it clean. No one else will undo my work. I will feel great to have it clean and in order."

Time-bound and trackable: "I can set a specific time to work on this task. This may bring it to completion. If not, I can return to it as often as necessary until it is complete."

As you engage with your practices, begin to notice the transformation within yourself: a little calmer, clearer, steadier and happier perhaps? Begin to notice the emerging foundations of strength which allow you to step free of the Fear Barrier. Notice the emergence of greater self-confidence, of Conscious Confidence.

Also, practice whenever you remember to do so. Your intention is to practice living with Conscious Confidence. The memory to practice is like someone giving you a gift. If you keep rejecting the gift of memory, then the giver will stop giving to you, in other words you won't remember to practice. When you do remember, say "Thank you" for that gift of memory. Then, practice immediately. The more frequently you receive the "gift" of memory with gratitude, the more often you will remember.

Conclusion

LIVING BEYOND LIMITS

"Get up! Stir yourself! Learn wisdom at the Master's feet.
A hard path the sages say, the sharp edge of a razor.
He who knows the soundless, odourless, tasteless, intangible,
formless, deathless, supernatural, undecaying, beginningless,
endless, unchangeable Reality, springs out of the mouth of Death."

—Shrī Purohit Swāmi and W. B. Yeats,
Katha Upanishad The Ten Principal Upanishads

Timeless wisdom is not just the province of the East. One of the wisest Western philosophers is Plato (c. 428 – 347 BCE). His allegory of the cave is one of the glories of the timeless wisdom of the West. It is a beautiful and succinct description of the human condition: trapped in illusion and then freed to make the journey from darkness to light, from illusion to reality, from the Fear Shadow to living with Conscious Confidence.

The Cave

Imagine prisoners in an underground cave, each with their ankles and neck shackled. The prisoners have been there since birth. They can't turn around, so they can only look at the back wall of the cave.

There is a blazing fire above and behind the prisoners. This throws shadows of them on the back wall.

Between the fire and the prisoners is a raised walkway with a screen along its length. People, carrying cut-out shapes of various objects such as animals, trees, flowers and buildings, walk up and down the walkway. Some of the shape-carriers talk and some remain silent, their voices echo off the back wall. So, the back wall of the cave has a passing parade of shadows.

Some of the prisoners discuss the order of these shadows. Their voices also echo off the back wall. The prisoners take the shadows to be real and believe the echoed voices are coming from the shadows, for they know of no other reality than what they can see on the back wall of the cave.

◆

Now imagine that one day someone enters the cave, and witnessing this strange scene, liberates one of the prisoners from his shackles. This liberator helps him to stand up, turn around and look at the blazing fire. At first the prisoner's eyes are in pain from the brightness of the light. Gradually they adjust and he can now see the objects being carried back and forth along the walkway. He realizes that these shapes are far more real than the shadows, which he previously took to be the only reality.

Now the liberator guides the freed prisoner past the fire to a steep narrow tunnel which leads out of the cave. The prisoner is again unable to see by being plunged into the darkness of the tunnel. The prisoner struggles to climb up the tunnel as it is steep and rocky. The liberator has to encourage and support him to keep going.

When the freed prisoner reaches the entrance to the cave, his eyes are dazzled by the brightness of the sunlight. He needs time for his eyes to adjust.

◆

At first, he can only see shadows cast on the ground of animals, trees, flowers and buildings. Then he can see them reflected in water and polished surfaces. Next his eyes can see these objects in moonlight, and eventually he can see them in the sunlight. Finally, he can see the sun itself.

Now the prisoner thinks back to his life in the cave, one of dark shadows. He remembers the awards and commendations that his fellow prisoners would give each other for knowing the order, shape and sounds of the shadows on the back wall. He feels no envy for his former friends and has no desire for their awards.

If he were to descend once more into the cave to free others, he would first find himself blinded again in the dim light. He would know that what he previously valued was in reality, valueless. The prisoners would be confused and unsettled by his speech. They would say to each other: "Look what has happened to him. He went up to this other place and has returned blind and ignorant of all our knowledge."

Were the freed prisoner to try to release someone from their bonds, they would surely now see him as a threat. They would turn against him out of fear that they too would be rendered blind and ignorant like him.

~ an allegory from Plato's *The Republic*, Book VII

This famous allegory of the cave illustrates the stages of the journey from darkness to light; from bondage to freedom; from being limited to expressing your full potential. It also contains a warning to take care when seeking to free others before they are ready!

An Invitation to Live beyond Limits

Most of us are like Plato's cave-dwellers. We find ourselves living in a limited state. Somehow the desire to be free, strong and confident arises in our hearts.

The journey to Conscious Confidence begins when we decide to come out from under the Fear Shadow, or when we decide that being a victim leads nowhere. With that realization we set out on a path where at each step we transcend one limitation, one fear, one negative thought after another. The journey is from limitation to limitlessness.

The consciousness within each of us is indeed limitless. It is ever-expanding because we are all constantly giving expression to it in our own unique and individual way. This unique self-expression is what we are born to offer the world.

Conscious Confidence is the foundation for this perfect unique self-expression. Conscious Confidence is the way to certainty, clarity and success. By using the timeless wisdom of Sanskrit, you too can find that Conscious Confidence.

What about You?

Throughout this book, you have read many stories. Now is your time to write your own story, your own journey, your own experience.

You are a limitless being. This is the message of all the wisdom traditions. Over the ages, in an unbroken thread, they have delivered this insight to humanity, that we are all truly limitless beings. You are capable of giving expression to your own limitless potential every moment of your life.

The teachers of timeless wisdom are speaking to you now—are you ready to hear?

Are you ready to step into a world of certainty, clarity and success—a world of Conscious Confidence? The door is open, the time is now, take the step.

> "We shall not cease from exploration
> And at the end of all our exploring
> Will be to arrive where we started
> And know the place for the first time."
>
> —T. S. Eliot, *Little Gidding*

APPENDICES

Glossary of Sanskrit Terms

In the order they appear in the book

sanskrita	संस्कृत	purified and perfectly formed
dhātu	धातु	verbal root
jñāna	ज्ञान	knowledge
Pāṇini	पाणिनि	Sanskrit scholar (4th–6th century BCE)
manas	मनस्	thinking mind aka 'monkey mind'
buddhi	बुद्धि	intellect or intelligence
chitta	चित्त	deep memory aka the heart
ahamkāra	अहंकार	the sense of existence: limited
aham	अहम्	the sense of existence: unlimited. I Am
sarva	सर्व	all
tattvamasi	तत्त्वमसि	Thou Art That
OM prema sarvān jayati	ॐ प्रेम सर्वान् जयति	OM Love Conquers All
seva	सेव	selfless service
santulana	संतुलन	balance
chetana	चेतन	being conscious
bhayam	भयमं	fear
mūlyam	मूल्यम्	taking root and growing strong
argha	अर्घ	respect, honor and worth
sthiti	स्थिति	point of view
bhāva	भाव	intent
vritti	वृत्ति	conduct

bali	बलि	a sacrificial offering
yajña – pashu	यज्ञपशु	a sacrificial animal
jetā	जेता	conqueror
varaṇa	वरण	choice; the act of choosing
shubhechchhā	शुभेच्छा	inspiration; good impulse
suvichāraṇā	सुविचारणा	application; true enquiry
tanumānasā	तनुमानसा	assimilation; refinement of the mind
sattvāpatī	सत्त्वापती	illumination; a state of clarity
asangsaktī	असंसक्ती	penetration with insight and detachment
padārthabhāvanī	पदार्थभावनी	dissolution and non-awareness of separate objects
turīya	तुरीय	completion in full realization of unity
dridha – pratyaya	दृढप्रत्यय	firm confidence
shraddhā	श्रद्धा	calm faith
nishchaya	निश्चय	conviction
ā – shā – bandha	आशाबन्ध	a strong desire for unity
pratyaya	प्रत्यय	firm belief and assurance
a – san – deha	असन्देह	uncluttered
a – san – digdha	असन्दिग्ध	clear and certain
a – saṃ – shaya	असंशय	awake and resolute
vi – shvāsa	विश्वास	freedom from fear
sam – ā – shvāsa	समाश्वास	to take courage
padam padam prati padam, arhati iti prātipadikam.	पदम् पदम् प्रति पदम्। अर्हति इति प्रातिपदिकम् ॥	Step by step; at every step awaits what is needed for that step.

Sanskrit Pronunciation Guide

Vowels

Short	Long
अ a Lisa	आ ā palm
इ i sit	ई ī seek
उ u bush	ऊ ū tool
ऋ ri river	ॠ rī reed
ऌ lri jewellery	(not used)
ए e prey	ऐ ai aisle
ओ o cope	औ au cloud

Consonants

Gutturals	क ka bike	ख kha blockhead	ग ga get	घ gha doghouse	ङ nga king
Palatals	च cha chat	छ chha beach-hat	ज ja jump	झ jha bridgehead	ञ ña onion
Cerebrals	ट ta true	ठ tha anthill	ड da drum	ढ dha redhair	ण ṇa band
Dentals	त ta tap	थ tha meat-hook	द da dark	ध dha adhere	न na not
Labials	प pa pan	फ pha cup-hook	ब ba big	भ bha abhor	म ma mop

Semi - Vowels

Palatal	Cerebral	Dental	Labial
य ya	र ra	ल la	व va

Sibilants

Gutteral	Palatal	Cerebral	Dental
ह ha	श sha shut	ष śha schnapps	स sa

Written either अं or अँ – is pronounced as either a 'n' or 'm' sound at the end of a word

अः – pronounced as a light 'h' sound at the end of a word

List of Practices

K = Key Practice   S = Starter Practice
I = Intermediate Practice   A = Advanced Practice

Stories, Contemporary Accounts, and Key Analogies

References

Bhagavad Gītā 6:13, from *The Geetā*. Put into English from the original Sanskrit by Shri Purohit Swāmi. London: Faber and Faber Ltd., 1955.

Chandogya Upanishad, The Ten Principal Upanishads. Transcribed into English by Shrī Purohit Swāmi and W. B. Yeats. London: Faber and Faber Ltd., 1937.

Eliot, T.S. "Little Gidding", from *Four Quartets*. Mariner Books, 1968.

Katha Upanishad, The Ten Principal Upanishads. Transcribed into English by Shrī Purohit Swāmi and W. B. Yeats. Faber and Faber Ltd., 1937.

Prashna Upanishad, The Ten Principal Upanishads. Transcribed into English by Shrī Purohit Swāmi and W. B. Yeats. Faber and Faber Ltd., 1937.

Shakespeare, William. *Hamlet* (Act 1, Scene 3), from *The Complete Works of Shakespeare*, 7th edition. London: Pearson Publishing, 2013.

_____. *Measure for Measure* (Act 1, Scene 4), from *The Complete Works of Shakespeare*, 7th edition. London: Pearson Publishing, 2013.

_____. *The Tempest* (Act 2, Scene 1), from *The Complete Works of Shakespeare*, 7th edition. London: Pearson Publishing, 2013.

Yoga, Vāsishta of Vālmīki (Book III, 118, 5 - 6). Edited by Ravi Prakash Arya. Parimal Publications, 1998.

INDEX

ACKNOWLEDGMENTS

The idea for this book came about through working with Dr. Pat Baccili. Dr. Pat reached out to me from the other side of the world. I had never heard of her before, but we connected and she helped me to get out of my own way by saying, "You know things I've never heard before." I am eternally grateful for Dr. Pat's vision, good humor and her open-heartedness.

Gail Torr of Galaxy Media has worked above and beyond to bring this book to fruition. Gail believed in the concept and contributed her considerable depth of knowledge and experience about the publishing world at each stage. I am deeply grateful for her professionalism with heart, and for her support and care throughout the process of producing this book. Thank you so much.

A big thank you goes to Nancy Peske, my developmental editor. I'm very grateful for the clarity that Nancy brought to the manuscript in countless ways. She spurred me on to think about some things from another perspective, and that's always a good thing.

Much appreciation goes to Elizabeth Ackerman for her help in the final preparation of the manuscript. I couldn't have done this without her skill, understanding and assistance.

I should like to acknowledge Sabine Weeke from Findhorn Press who recognized the jewel of Sanskrit and wanted it to have the starring role in the book.

My gratitude also goes to Michael Hawkins, the fine editor for Findhorn Press. Michael read the manuscript with great care and attention and gave me such valuable feedback and confirmation. I very much appreciated his sensitive insights and praise.

A special acknowledgement goes to my dear friend and calligrapher Deirdre Hassed. Thank you for the beautiful hand-written elements in the cover design and for your sweet encouragement.

My heartfelt gratitude goes to all the teachers of philosophy, Sanskrit and meditation that have been my guides and inspiration since the tender age of ten.

Finally, there are no words that can really express my gratitude to my husband Gilbert. Gil is my greatest fan and yet he'll always bring his rapier-like intellect to bear on anything that isn't clear, and I certainly need that!

About the Author

Photo by David Mane

Sarah Mane is a Sanskrit scholar with a particular interest in the wisdom of Sanskrit as a practical means to life-mastery. Previously a teacher and school executive, today she is a transformational and executive coach. Sarah lives in Australia.

For more information see her website:
https://consciousconfidence.com

FINDHORN PRESS

Life-Changing Books

Learn more about us and our books at
www.findhornpress.com

For information on the Findhorn Foundation:
www.findhorn.org